WHY
VEGAN

Second edition published 1995 by Heretic Books Ltd
P O Box 247, London N6 4BW, England
phone +181 341 7818 fax +181 341 7467
First edition published 1985 by GMP Publishers Ltd
World copyright © Kath Clements 1985 & 1995

A CIP record is available from the British Library

ISBN 0 946097 30 5

Distributed in EU by Central Books
99 Wallis Road, London E9 5LN, England
phone +181 986 4854 fax +181 533 5821

Distributed in NA by Inbook
P O Box 120470, East Haven, CT 06512, USA
phone +203 467 5434 fax +203 469 7697

Distributed in Australia by Bulldog Books
P O Box 155, Broadway, NSW 2007, Australia
phone +2 550 5577 fax +2 550 5789

Printed in EU by Norhaven A/S,
5 Agerlandsvej, DK-8800 Viborg, Danmark

WHY
VEGAN

The Ethics of Eating & the Need for Change

KATH CLEMENTS

heretic books

LONDON

CONTENTS

CHAPTER ONE

WHY VEGAN?

Food is a subject close to everyone's heart, whether we admit it or not. As well as fulfilling one of our basic appetites, it should be a happy subject with its connotations of good times and celebrations. But in our world of hunger and starvation on the one hand, and chronic illness and eating disorders on the other, food these days is not necessarily the happy subject it could be. The first part of this book is about our own responsibility, through the food we eat, for the use or abuse of Earth's resources. The book is an attempt to persuade and enable more people to adopt a diet which excludes animal products, so that we can improve our own health and the health of our planet, as well as making a stand against the huge imbalance in food distribution throughout the world. The problems outlined in the opening chapters may fill you with despair, but read on — you will learn how to become part of the solution!

(i) Vegan — The Word

The word "vegan" was coined in 1945 in Britain by the newly-formed Vegan Society, to describe those who avoid animal products for food, clothing and other consumer products. (The word is simply a shortening of the word "vegetarian" and the root word in Latin for all the words derived from "vegetable" means to quicken or enliven.) There were numbers of people who took the step for their own ethical reasons (we shall never know how many) with no knowledge of the Vegan Society or this new word, and some who were glad to find out about it later, for its support and guidance. During the years before veganism became as widespread as it is today, many were helped and enlightened by the Vegan Society, including myself.

Many thousands now follow a vegan diet without the need for special guidance, without the feeling of taking a fairly drastic step, and even without joining the Vegan Society. The negative connotations which the word has sometimes been given — mainly in circles where uninformed condemnation or ridicule are the only line of defence for "traditional" eating habits — are now fading fast as the second and third generations of healthy vegans are standing up to be counted.

Vegans, of course, are individuals with their own ideals and varying reasons for adopting their diet and lifestyle. This little book is an attempt to explain the main reasons, from one vegan's viewpoint, and to suggest some ideas about food and meals.

Veganism is not about cats' homes and being kind to furry animals, nor about living in cloud cuckoo-land where nature's cycle of destruction and creation can somehow be avoided. Vegans do not imagine that their food bypasses every possibility of death and suffering for the animal kingdom. The grain fields needed for the bread we eat rob many animals of their natural habitats and mean that many more are killed as pests. It is not necessarily compassion for animals alone which leads people to veganism. Veganism is about having a consistent approach to human rights and animal rights, ecology and world food problems. It is a very important subject indeed, since each of us is responsible through what we consume for the management of the Earth's resources, and ultimately for peaceful coexistence with others on the planet.

(ii) World Food

A prime reason for veganism is the desperate nature of the world food situation. The threat of destruction of the world through atomic fission or climatic change hovers over us and we fear for our children's future, yet millions are already watching their children starve in conditions similar to a post-holocaust famine. Despite the fact that the world production of grain has not recently fallen much below 1 kg per day for every person alive, twelve to thirteen million children die each year through malnutrition (about one every two seconds as you read this); that is the equivalent of a Hiroshima every three days. This generation of Europeans should now be thoroughly aware of the extreme poverty of many other nations, though profiteers and politicians in our own country encourage us unceasingly to hope for even higher standards of living for ourselves.

It is the over-consumption of meat, eggs and dairy products in the West that underlies the inequitable distribution of the world's food resources, because as well as feeding ourselves, we in the affluent countries are feeding a huge population of farm animals (fig. 1).

Figure 1

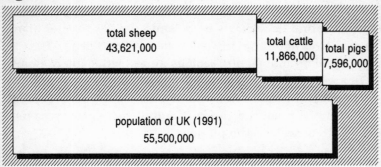

Ministry of Agriculture figures of June 1992 — supplied by the Meat and Livestock Commission (note that these totals exclude chicken and fish)

In Britain, as can be seen from *fig. 1,* the population of farm animals exceeds that of humans. On a global scale, "there are currently 1.28 billion cattle populating the Earth. They take up nearly 24 per cent of the land mass of the planet and consume enough grain to feed hundreds of millions of people."[1]

According to a recent Vegetarian Society booklet, the world's cattle consume a quantity of feed equal to the calorific needs of nearly double the human population of the planet. Colossal commercial interests on the one hand, and blinkered table habits on the other, encourage us to continue in ignorance of these facts. The facts are that our farm animals are routinely fed on vegetable protein suitable for direct human consumption, and often their feedstuff is grown in countries where the majority of the population is malnourished. As much as 40 % of the world's grain is used as cattle feed in addition to 40–50% of its fish and 25–40% of its dairy products.[2] On average, a family in the rich world will consume five times more grain (including feed grain) than a family in the poor world.

(iii) The Meat and Milk Myth

Animal products are not an essential part of our diet, though the large majority of British people are convinced that meat, milk and eggs are natural, healthy and necessary to sustain human life. But farming has become extremely unnatural and its products far less healthy in order to feed our large urban populations on animal protein. The belief in the almost magical properties of meat and milk is deeply rooted in our culture.

There are social and historical reasons for this, dating back to times when only the rich could afford to eat much meat. People ate meat less often and their small portion was indeed the richest thing on their plates. Farms were smaller and used organic methods which are no longer profitable, so the meat was a chemically different product. And history shows that people have eaten increasingly large amounts of meat. From being a rare treat for ordinary people in mediaeval times, consumption of meat increased over the centuries with the rising expectations of working people, especially when in the New World countless acres of prairies were opened up in the 19th century. We now have an extreme situation where someone might eat meat three times a day. Throughout the world, meat eating has symbolised the rich life of the old ruling classes; now everyone wants it and the poor who go hungry are not outside the castle gates but in the economically deprived countries which provide our primary products.

The historical reasons for this situation date back to the 19th century British taste for fatty beef, developed at a time when surplus corn in the New World could be used in the huge feedlots where cattle were herded prior to slaughter. Large-scale feeding of grain to cattle was a comparatively new development in agriculture and one that has had an enormous effect on land use and food distribution worldwide.

In fact the demand for meat is behind the whole colossus of the food industry and especially grain production. But the belief in meat and milk is nothing but a myth, a massive con-trick perpetuated by the huge corporations involved.[3]

Governments have traditionally bolstered the farming industry, nowhere more so than in post-war Britain and especially in recent times with the Common Agricultural Policy. The CAP uses over half of the total EU budget (10% of which goes astray through corruption according to the European Court of Auditors Report 22/4/92) and enables farmers to sell their products at a good price almost regard-less of demand. This policy works to the detriment of producers in the developing countries, whose governments cannot afford to subsidise them to compete on the world market. It has also led to surpluses in our own country which have now been reduced to the still staggering amounts of 15,713,000 tonnes of cereals, 361,000 tonnes of butter and 607,000 tonnes of beef (UK figures October 1991). So, added to the grain and energy costs of producing meat are the enormous costs of storing the stuff. Predictably, the latest reforms to the CAP (May 1992) with the set-aside policy and generous compensation to farmers for producing nothing, will work to the benefit of the more powerful and shrewd farmers.

The National Farmers Union is an extremely powerful body, and it is no accident that many politicians are also farmers. Geoffrey Cannon (see book list) researched MPs' interests during 1986 and found that 250 Members of Parliament had connections with the food industry. Cabinet ministers are not expected to have direct links with indus-try although they can continue to own farms!

In farming, there are no constraints on over-production, as there are with other industries of national importance. On the contrary, massive amounts of tax-payers' money in addition to grants from Europe are spent on bolstering the meat industry, with schemes such as the beef special premium scheme, the suckler cow premium and the hill compensatory allowance (so that we all pay for meat whether we eat it or not). In the UK even small farmers benefit from rate and tax exemptions, including VAT. Government subsidies which began in wartime to keep food prices down now exist largely to promote the producers' interests and so far no amount of consumer pressure has lessened the influence of the industry over official policymakers.

At the moment, the food economy is geared to meat production whether we like it or not, and we are all paying for it with public money. But the system relies heavily on imports — our "home produced" meat is in fact no more British than a car assembled from imported components. It worsens the imbalance of actual food consumption between the rich and the poor countries and underlies the inequitable distribution of resources.

Now for a closer look at the inefficiency, in real terms, of modern farming, and at some of the powerful interests that keep it going.

CHAPTER TWO

THE FOOD INDUSTRY

"Successive governments in Britain have taken the advice above all of the giant food and chemical manufacturers. This explains British food policy, and also the British farming landscape."
— Geoffrey Cannon, *The Politics of Food*

"If we were all vegetarians and shared our food equally, the world could support six billion.... But if one-third of our calories came from animal products, as in North America today, then it would only be able to sustain 2.5 billion." — Sir Crispin Tickell, former UN Ambassador, speaking at the annual meeting of the British Association for the Advancement of Science, August 1991.
(World population has now passed 5 billion.)

(i) Economy

That meat is a wasteful way of producing food protein is beyond doubt. Weight for weight, there is only about a 10 per cent conversion rate from plant to animal protein (less if you count how much of the product is unusable or wasted) which means that it takes an awful lot of plant material to produce a certain amount of steak, eggs or milk.

Figures vary, of course, but it is noticeable how often this ratio of approximately ten to one keeps recurring in studies of food returns. For instance, using body weight as a measure, it would take ten kilos of fish to make a person gain one kilo in weight. The fish would have consumed 100 kilos of shrimp and worms, and the shrimps and worms, 1,000 kilos of plankton. So one kilo of the person's body weight represents one tonne of matter two steps further down the food chain! (This example is used by Kit Pedler in his book *The Quest for Gaia*.) Again, using land as a measure of efficiency, cereals produce five times as much protein as meat, peas and beans ten times more and spinach twenty-six times more.[4]

Another estimate has shown that soya beans can produce 260 kg of protein per acre, lucerne 675 kg per acre and prime grade beef only 49 kg per acre.[5] *(see fig. 2)*

So it takes a lot more land to feed a meat eater than it does a vegetarian. In a world where farm land is at a premium, and the retention of what is left of natural forests has become absolutely crucial, it would make sense to make the most of the agricultural land that we have. Whereas the reality at present is that in Britain 90% of the 46 million acres of agricultural land is devoted directly or indirectly to livestock, 29 million acres is used for grazing and two thirds of the crops grown on the arable land are used for feed.[6]

Water is another precious resource and to produce just a pound of grainfed steak requires hundreds of gallons of water to irrigate feed crops. One pound of soya beans needs 480 gallons of water in production, whereas one pound of beef has taken 2,464 gallons, according to the US Water Education Foundation.

Figure 2
**Number of people that can be fed from
10 acres of land:**

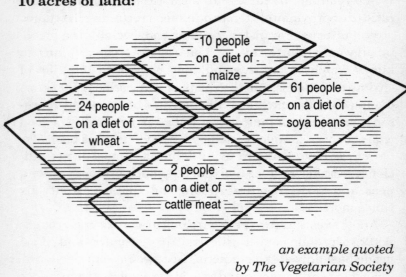

*an example quoted
by The Vegetarian Society*

In terms of our farming industry's efficiency, there is also to be considered the cost in energy of shipping animal feed halfway around the world and of running the intensive units which comprise the majority of modern farms. It is not certain how much longer our banks or our environment can bear this cost.

The UK trade deficit in food and drink now stands at £6 billion.[7] If the balance of payments is a concern of British politicians, they could do worse than reduce the amount we spend on imported animal feedstuffs. In 1982 the EC imported 14 million tonnes of grain just to feed animals. Britain alone imports 4 million of the 14 million tonnes of grain to feed livestock each year.[8] Yet most of our farmland is already devoted to livestock (we import most of the wheat for our bread from the US). Worse still, much of the protein we import for animal feed comes from countries where the poor go hungry (manioc from Thailand, soya from Brazil, fish meal from Peru and soya beans and oilseeds from India, for example). During a fowl pest scare, I read in my local paper of "rice bran and wheat bran ingredients imported from Pakistan, the Far East and other places" which had become contaminated at Liverpool. That chicken feed should travel so far seems absurd especially when we don't even need the end product:

> "Food imports are, in fact, unnecessary. Our farm land is productive enough to support 250 million people on a vegetarian diet."
> — *British Medical Journal* July 1977
> *(The population of the UK is under 60 millions.)*

This would seem to be the pattern in countries which become industrialised. For instance, Egypt was self-sufficient in food in 1970 but now imports 70 per cent of its food. The former Soviet States also import huge amounts of grain to satisfy the demand for meat, which has ultimately left them at the mercy of the world's largest exporter — the USA.

(ii) The Big Boys

> "The food producers' monopoly exceeds the oil producers' monopoly."
> — US Assistant Secretary of State 1974

The problem is huge and so are the forces behind it. 600 million tons of grain is fed to livestock today in our world where, according to WHO statistics, 40 to 60 million people each year die from hunger and related diseases.[9] The grain shipments occasionally made to famine-stricken parts of the world are a worthless fraction of the amounts we store and import to feed our immense population of farm animals. Huge corporations like Nestles, Unilever, Hillsdown Holdings, Associated British Foods and H J Heinz are in control of the rearing, transport and slaughter of the billions of head of livestock on farms and ranches today. Often farmers are contract growers and what they grow bears little relation to local demand.

But the farmers themselves are not in control of the industry; in Britain at least, decisions controlling food policy are taken in closed committees, governed by the Official Secrets Act! Consumers are not involved in the committees which make important policy decisions, but representatives of the food industry — as opposed to disinterested nutritionists — certainly are. Britain's continuing ill-health is a sad testimony to this. During the 1970's and 80's the public awareness of the link between saturated fats and heart disease could be said to have come about despite official policy, rather than because of it.[10]

The National Advisory Council on Nutrition Education, set up in 1979, was so obstructed by the agriculturalists and food manufacturers that its final report became too obscure to be of much use to the general public. No effective dietary education took place and heart disease continued to take its toll. British statistics provided a control by which other countries could measure their success in reducing coronary heart disease, and Britain still leads the world in this statistic if nothing else. This is what happens when leaders of the food industry are involved with politics at the highest level.[11]

In fact, in the ten years or so since the COMA (Committee on Medical Aspects of Food) report has been officially recognised and its advice on sugar and animal fat promoted, our fat and sugar consumption has hardly changed; this is largely because of the heavy use of fats and sugars in processed foods and the fact that the industry has encouraged a "two tier" system by offering "health" products at a premium. The poor are still eating rubbish.

The British Nutrition Foundation, one of the supposed guardians of our health, with the stated aim of spreading the "scientific" and "objective" word about health, is itself largely a creation of the food industry. It was set up in 1967 as a forum for senior people from science, government and the food industry and it has an influence on British policy similar to that of the Food and Drink Federation in the USA.

However, in its 1982 report, *Implementation of Dietary Guidelines: Obstacles and Opportunities*, the following passage is found:

> "Any consideration of national dietary guidelines must take account of this economic colossus (the food industry). . . . The prime industries provide employment for over two million people, have huge sums invested in them and are a major factor in the economic health of the nation. . . . Simply to say 'let there be substantially less sugar or butter', for example, would have far-reaching economic implications worldwide."

The organisation is condemned by its own words as the vested interests are admitted. To be fair, however, it must be said that the vegetarian movement has not always grasped the nettle of the economic implications of the destruction of a whole industry, for this is what it is really about. Just as the abolitionists of previous centuries had to counter the argument that the world economy would collapse without slavery, similar arguments must now be faced around the food industry.

Meanwhile the food mountains and lakes continue to flourish, not only in Britain but in America as well. Below the ground in Kansas City is the country's largest "Commercial Distribution Center", where trucks line up to dump endless tons of cereal grains which cannot immediately be sold. Indeed it was the huge American grain surpluses in the post-war years that actually gave rise to the burger industry — the perfect way to condense and transform a cheap food into an expensive one. And over here, farmers have removed even more of our irreplaceable countryside over the past two decades because of the artificially high price of wheat in the EU. Of course, these lunacies are not caused purely by our meat-based diet; but operations which rely on the shipment of such huge amounts of feed for livestock, where large investments are involved, are bound to get out of hand. And we can be certain that handsome profits have been made whilst the food mountains have been accumulating.

CHAPTER THREE

DOWN ON THE FARM

"World meat production has almost quadrupled since 1950. In nations such as Belgium and France, animals produce more waste than the land can absorb. Over-grazing has affected 73% of the world's rangelands and pasture expansion is the single leading cause of Latin American deforestation."
— *Worldwatch Institute* July 1991

(i) Factory Farming

Despite the absurdities of Western food production, there are still many who think that modern developments are our main hope of feeding our huge populations. Factory farming, for instance, was hailed as a necessary evil which was to alleviate food shortages by confining farming operations into a smaller space. But confined animals take a much higher proportion of their food from good arable land than do animals which roam in the fields. In close confinement, the health and vitality of the animals suffer, and so does the product. Reliance on drugs and additives to combat infection increases artificial residues in the products, and heightens the risk to the consumer as bacteria become immune to antibiotics. This is clearly seen at the present time, when the number of reported cases of food poisoning in the UK quadrupled in the four years up to 1990.

And this is the product which the myth encourages us to consider the mainstay of our lives! Also, factory farms maintain their controlled environments by heavy dependence on hardware and energy resources. Even in less intensive farming, the total cost of animal husbandry in fuel and water is immense compared with simply producing crops.

(ii) Dairy Farming

But surely, they say, we can still have milk and other dairy produce, since cows produce it so abundantly it must make good sense for us to drink it. Unfortunately (for the cows) this is not the case, since, as with all mammals including ourselves, lactation occurs only in the period following the birth of a calf. A cow gives as milk only about one tenth of the protein she eats, and what she eats these days is not all in the form of cellulose (grass) which she is "designed" to digest; it is in the form of concentrated cereal protein pellets which lead to serious metabolic problems as we shall see later.

Partly by such artificial feeding and partly by selective breeding, the annual production of a typical dairy cow has been increased from 1,500 litres of milk in 1950 to over 5,000 litres in 1983 (more than ten times as much as the calf would have drunk had it been left to suckle).[12] Mere grazing in the meadows does not produce such yields. The methods of modern dairy farming are a very expensive way of producing a product which is in surplus.

The dairy industry is really part and parcel of the beef industry, with 80 per cent of UK beef being a by-product of dairy farms. The calf which each cow has to produce each year to maintain her milk supply will either be slaughtered very early for veal, or it will go to a veal farm or a beef herd;

a minority of females become part of another dairy herd. Public ignorance of these basic facts, together with wishful thinking, must be one of the triumphs of advertising in the modern world. It is much more comfortable to believe in the existence of contented farm animals who are only too happy to "give" us their milk etc. than to picture the realities of the dairy industry.

Dairy surpluses are offloaded in various bizarre ways. Flavoured drinks are often tried, and fail. At Haslington, near Crewe, a factory was switched in 1984 to converting whey for use by the pharmaceutical trade in pill-making. In Devon, the stuff is simply dumped over the fields.[13] In recent years, whey has popped up in various surprising places in foods which are not normally associated with milk, as habitual readers of food labels will realise. In terms of the Earth's resources, the dairy industry is responsible for a colossal amount of wastage.

(iii) Animal Waste

One aspect of the wastage is the slurry produced by the dairy farms. Advocates of animal farming say that animal manure is necessary to keep the soil in good heart. Indeed, in the natural course of events both animal and human waste would be returned as nutrients to the soil by the process of decay. But so much animal waste is produced in intensive farming that it is impossible to return it to the land locally and it is either transported elsewhere, stored in dangerous slurry lakes or simply burned to create a different form of pollution.

Far from being good for the land, modern husbandry is a major pollutant of the country's water systens. In a typical year (1982) 2,523 cases of pollution from farms were reported to water authorities in this country[14] and many more no doubt went unreported. Animal slurry from farms wreaks havoc with the wildlife and fish of our rivers by stripping oxygen from the water. A dairy cow produces 9 gallons of slurry per day and one dairy unit has the pollution potential of a small town. In addition, the liquid wastes created by silage (the modern answer to the hay loft) can be 200 times worse than sewage in terms of the damage done to a river.[15] Other chemical spin-off, from fertilisers and pesticides, has wrecked ecosystems and is responsible for the alarming amounts of nitrates in our drinking water.

Pollution of the land and waterways is not the only hazard of animal farming: in recent years it has become obvious that there are implications on a global scale. Vast herds of cattle breathe out carbon dioxide and belch out the much more potent gas methane, which is 20-25 times as powerful as CO_2 as a greenhouse gas and described by James Lovelock in the 1990 Schumacher lecture as "probably the most dangerous substance we are injecting into the atmosphere". So the 31 million acres currently used as permanent pasture for the cows which each typically produce about 200 litres of methane per day are a serious factor in accelerating global warming. This uncomfortable truth has not yet been faced by the meat-and-two-veg brigade and for vigorously pointing it out we have to thank Kathleen Jannaway, author of such works as *Abundant Living in the Coming Age of the Tree* and founder of the Movement for Compassionate Living (see contacts list).

In addition to contributing to the build-up of greenhouse gases, animal farming is a major source of air pollution. Animal waste is one of the main sources of ammonium, which directly damages plants and causes acid rain. A 1991 Worldwatch Institute report states that ammonia from livestock manures in Holland causes more acid rain damage than its cars or factories. (In 1992 the Dutch government announced incentives to persuade farmers to turn from dairy to energy farming with modern windmills.)

(iv) Healthy Soil and Healthy Landscape

A common myth, hedged in by nostalgia and tradition, is that soil needs animal manure to grow healthy crops. But of course human waste is obviously available in large quantities to provide organic fertiliser and there are several projects in the UK which demonstrate how this can be done.[16] It cannot be done on a large scale at present because our sewage is so full of contaminants like heavy metals from industrial pollution. The hygienic recycling of human waste is well within technological capability but as yet there is no money in it.

Animal waste is, however, not necessarily a vital ingredient of crop growing. On a 32 hectare farm near Strasbourg, for example, organic stockless farming was successfully practised for over twelve years, and with crop rotation and green manuring rye, wheat and beans were grown in abundance without the use of animal manure.[17] In this country there are many gardens and allotments which use "veganic" methods, that is, gardening without artificial chemicals or animal products like manure, bone meal etc. (see Bibliography). Compost making is the mainstay of good gardening and is in fact a much more direct way of feeding the soil.

The nutrients and "body" contained in manures "can be readily obtained from simply composting or fermenting the vegetative and protein feed directly without having to grow livestock".[18] And if a soil is deficient in minerals they can be added in the form of ground rocks, seaweed, etc. Far from muck being the "magic" that is claimed, it actually represents a net loss of soil value because of the energy that has been burned up during the life of the animal producing it. The "muck" is not a natural and local product but in fact comes from the country of origin of the grain fed to the animal.

To see the case for veganic methods, only contrast the delight of spreading sweet-smelling compost over your garden with the unpleasant experience of being near a field where muck-spreading is taking place. Traditionally, animal manure has been the method of maintaining soil fertility on Britain's smaller mixed farms, but those days are a long way behind us. Nowadays, the typical farm has reached 4,000 acres in extent, with one third of the total number of farms in Britain occupying nine-tenths of the agricultural land.[19] Soil fertility is maintained courtesy of ICI, and animal slurry is an embarrassment to the farmer.

In a situation where there was no animal farming, soil fertility could be easily maintained by compost growing, crop rotation, green manuring and the careful recycling of human waste. If we did not "grow" animals, our "overcrowded" island would have no difficulty feeding itself on a vegan diet, as was shown by a study undertaken under the auspices of Professor Watkin Williams, head of the Department of Agriculture and Botany at Reading University (this is also explored in Kenneth Mellanby's *Can Britain Feed Itself?* — see Bibliography).

The vegan landscape would include many trees as a prime renewable source of food as well as fuel, animal-free fibres and building materials. Trees once covered almost the whole of our landscape up to a height of 600 metres; much of the traditional English landscape, far from being "natural", is the product of the enclosure acts in the 17th and 18th centuries — some of the most cruel legislation in history. Tree planting is of course vital in maintaing ecosystems and the health of the planet but what is not so widely known is that trees are also a prime renewable source of food, providing legumes (not yet in the UK), fruits and nuts. For instance, "the yield per acre of well-managed hazel trees may reach at least two tons, though average yields still range from 6–10 cwts per acre".[20]

In fact, a larger amount of food per acre can be produced by tree-growing than by any other means. Walnuts, for instance, have an astonishingly high food value and supply many essential nutrients. "An acre of walnuts will supply more than 1,000 lbs of shelled nuts . . . this is 20 times the amount that the same acre would yield in beef. The protein quality of the nuts would be as great as in beef and of superior quality".[21] In addition, the food technology that has developed around the soya bean could be adapted to local crops, and low tech protein extraction from green leaves is already taking place commercially in the UK.[22]

By biomass fermentation, "all required liquid fuel could be obtained from 17 per cent of the UK's land area and all gas from 15 per cent" (Professor David Hall of King's College, giving evidence at the Windscale Enquiry of 1977). The manufacture of fuel alcohol on a large scale has already been put into practice in Brazil (unfortunately in this case, only running cars for the rich). According to Professor Hall, this time addressing the Vegan Society in May 1984, all of the world's economically extractable coal, oil and gas only have an energy content equal to that of the trees now growing in the world.

Wood is already being used to make petrol substitutes especially in the US. Farmers in the UK are using coppiced wood for on-site production of electricity, growing it on "set-aside" land.

British farmers, the most conservative of groups, are now asking for change. At the annual meeting of the NFU in February 1992, farmers demanded incentives to help them grow crops which could be turned into diesel oil, plastics, paper and fuel for power stations. Starch from sugar beet and cereals could form the basis of a bio-degradable plastic, and straw, willow and other coppice woods could be grown to power electricity generating plants. Oilseed rape is already being grown in the UK to produce a "green" bio-diesel oil, which when burned is less damaging than conventional fossil fuels. How much more could be done if we did not waste so much of our farm land on animal feed.

(v) Necessary Changes

Instead of constantly searching for ways in which to exploit animals ever more horrifically, scientists could be researching these promising new areas. But the merciless exploitation of animals will cease only when the market for their flesh has finally disappeared. The industry is strong enough at present to bolster itself with massive advertising campaigns, but the fact that advertising for meat is now actually taking place is really a good sign for the vegetarian movement.

If consumers create even stronger market demands and refuse to be brainwashed by the efforts of the Meat and Livestock Commission, the ingenious farmers will just have to respond by producing every type of cereal, vegetable, fruit and pulse that our climate allows. They could find new sources of income and opportunities for cash crop growing and syndicate operation, and our government could be subsidising healthy foods instead of unhealthy ones.

CHAPTER FOUR

ECOLOGICAL ASPECTS OF FOOD PRODUCTION

"Animal abuse, whether in farms, vivisection laboratories, in the wild, or in our own homes, is not a peripheral, soft issue that can be divorced from more heavily publicised worries over ecological destruction. Animal cruelty is the most decisive evidence of our grotesque and, ultimately, self-destructive triumphalism in respect of the rest of creation." — Andrew Tyler

(i) The Land

Our civilisation has disrupted the traditional cultures of three continents to fuel our rampant consumerism. At the same time, our rich Western diet, which concentrates on animal farming, has drastically changed the appearance of our own landscapes and those of half the world.

Animal farming is sometimes defended on the grounds that animals can feed on grasslands and in hill country unsuitable for arable crops, and on plants unsuitable for human digestion, so that they have a valid place in the ecology of farming. However, in many parts of the world large-scale grazing of animals has been disastrous for the local ecology. The results of over-grazing are clearly seen on our own moorlands, whilst at the other end of the scale, the Sahara Desert itself is largely a creation of over-grazing. And in Brazil, for instance, huge cattle ranches take up some of the most fertile soil whilst even more irreplaceable rainforest land is being destroyed in order to produce meat for American beefburgers (though tropical grazing land thus created has a life of ten years at very best); and yet 60 per cent of Brazilians are malnourished. In other Latin American countries the situation is similar, with exports of beef cattle having increased five-fold.

In Britain as elsewhere, instead of grazing animals, we could replant trees where forests once grew and, unlike grazing animals, these would protect soil from erosion and maintain the water table, preventing both drought and swamping, and renewing the purity of the air and the whole fertility of the land and viability of our large populations upon it. Animal manure is not necessary for soil fertility as long as crop rotation is practiced and "wastes" are returned. On a small scale, putting a goat or two on a piece of rough land is an easy way out for people with no real love and understanding of the land; at the other end of the scale, hill farming as it is now practiced is an absurdity which costs us millions in government subsidies.

All our energy needs as well as food needs could be met from agricultural land, even with our relatively high population, if animal farming could be brought to an end. After all, grazing animals are the enemies of stable plant cover of the soil. Plants and especially trees are our most precious renewable resource, providing fuel, food, textiles, cosmetics and almost anything else that human ingenuity might devise.

As well as removing the wasteful and polluting stockfarming industries, a plant-based economy could gradually ease and then remove altogether our dependence on the unsustainable and more polluting mineral fuels. We could have an industrial revolution all over again, but this time based on sustainable and cleaner resources. Reclothing our land with trees has stunning social, economic and political implications!

(ii) The Sea

Unfortunately, our dependence on animal products has not only disfigured and impoverished the land, but has drastically denatured the sea as well. Even some "vegetarians" will eat fish, saying perhaps to their conscience that sea fish at least are free-range. But the shoals of herring of our folk songs were almost fished out of existence prior to the ban in the late seventies, and now other once-common species are facing extinction too. Though the EC ministers did at last reach an agonising agreement on fishing limits in December 1991, environmentalists claim that the effect will be far too little; we are eating endangered species along with our chips. And the result of all this is that the most plentiful fish available in UK markets these days are not cod, haddock and plaice but exotic species that may have come from almost any part of the world except the North Sea.

Fishing in Britain has been an uncertain occupation since the market for fish has become global big business, but the plight of the fishermen is not half so serious as that of marine life itself. For decades now fishing fleets, notably the Japanese, have been using huge nets which stretch across hundreds of miles of ocean at a time, trapping as well as the fish millions of sea birds and marine animals in the fine mesh. Japan has now agreed to follow other nations and ban driftnets by the end of 1992, but again this is too little, too late.

Farmers, at least, sow before they reap. Fishermen only reap, and that with cruelty on an almost unimaginable scale. As well as the obvious abuses involved in driftnet fishing, there is trawling, which ploughs the ocean bed often several times each year, destroying acres of flora and fauna. There is also fixed net fishing, where the huge invisible nets are fixed over large areas of sea bed for several days and on being drawn up, after the more valuable fish have been removed, are thrown back along with the unwanted trapped fish to pollute the sea. And there is commercial long line fishing, which impales fish on 3,000 hooks in lines up to 100km long, in order to lift them to their slow suffocation, which may take several hours. (After the publication of the Medway report in 1980 we can be in no doubt that all vertebrates, warm or cold blooded, are capable of feeling pain.) There is no legistlation to control the slaughter of fish, as there is with all other animals used as food.[23]

Factory farming of fish, too, is extremely damaging to the environment and accounts for a high proportion of fish on our supermarket shelves. There are now over 1,000 fish farms in Britain which produce over 44,000 tonnes of fish per year. A fish farm with stocks of 300 tonnes will produce the same amount of sewage as a town of 100,000 people and this will contain large doses of the chemicals which are used to control disease at the farms.[24] And in many developing countries fish farms are appearing too (particularly for prawns and shrimps — not technically fish), as more traditional food markets collapse. But this is a capital-intensive, low labour industry which mainly benefits the large corporations which provide the capital; it has a devastating effect on the ecology of coastal waters.[25]

"Fishing" on such a horrific scale is what it is all about if we are to feed fish to our vast urban populations. And the saddest part of commercial fishing, as we have seen, is that 40-50 per cent of the world's catch is used only to fatten livestock or factory farmed fish! This situation should not continue if we respect the ecology of the oceans as vital to the atmospheric composition and climatic stability of the planet. What the sea can actually give us is wind and water power, which are infinitely renewable.

(iii) The Future

Many scientists would now agree that our best hope lies in reclothing the Earth with trees and returning to a plant-based economy. And yet the poorer nations are being encouraged by the multinational food companies to aspire to a Western-type diet with a heavy use of animal protein. Intensive farming, relying of course on Western-produced technology, is being tried in many parts of the poor world. As well as taking grain virtually from the mouths of the poor, such developments can only mean disaster for the world's resources. Attempts to make a meat-based diet available for everyone can only destroy the environment.

On the other hand, it is not conducive to harmony and peace between nations to have such a diet available as at present only to the rich nations, for whom meat eating has become a deeply entrenched habit. A lifetime of conditioning from all sides has encouraged us to think of meat and milk as central to our diet. But if ecological or economic factors do not encourage us to rethink this, then perhaps some healthy self-interest and knowledge of nutrition may do so.

CHAPTER FIVE

NUTRITION

"We are primates, and primates are all vegetarians with only rare meat consumption by certain species. All the protein, minerals, and vitamins the human body needs are easily obtained from plant sources. The taste for meats and other fatty foods is like a substance abuse to which we are addicted early in life. While we have been struggling — and failing — to cure heart diseases and cancer, their primary causes are right under our noses, on the dinner table." — Dr Neal Barnard, President, Physicians Committee for Responsible Medicine

(i) Our Natural Food

The fact is that our bodies seem to be "designed" to be vegetarian, or, more accurately, like the great apes, to digest a diet of fruit, nuts and shoots. We are not properly adapted to the consumption of flesh, far less the milk of other animals.

I once watched the rotund botanist on a TV chat show, spouting a typical carnivore's diatribe on the lines of "Haw

haw, vegetarians have got it all wrong — anyone can see that horses' and cows' guts are far different from ours — we can't live on vegetables like the puny vegetarians, haw haw. . . ." This was gross misinformation from one who ought to know better and it is typical of the brain-washing that happens regularly. The meat myth is strong indeed when a scientist, watched by millions, can get away with such rubbish.

It is true that we are not like the herbivores, as anyone can see without even the need to slit one open to observe its copious entrails, developed for dealing with cellulose. Obviously we can't live on grass. But far from being akin to nature's carnivores, the pattern of organs in our bodies and the composition of our blood are identical to those of the great apes, i.e. the larger tail-less monkeys such as chimpanzees and gorillas.

Though modern-day researchers cannot be sure of human origins, it does seem likely that the traditional view of early man as a violent hunter has got it very wrong. The picture which has filled the early pages of many a school history book, of a club-bearing brute battering to death his next meal, is completely fictional, though it may serve as a fitting model for the origins of a culture which has developed through belligerent self-interest. This is perfectly in line with the old school of history which has battles as its main landmarks, offering to young people stories of extreme brutality and selfishness (like the Wars of the Roses) as our "heritage" rather than as something of which we should feel deeply ashamed.

As regards the origins of humankind, it is much more likely that we began as frugivorous creatures and took to flesh-eating only as a result of a migration to inhospitable regions, or a catastrophe like an ice age which removed plant cover. Or perhaps it was the stress of territorial threat from other species which made early humans turn to violence and flesh-eating, as has been observed with our cousins the chimpanzees who in rare circumstances, like encroaching human settlements, camera crews and the like, have been found to kill to eat.

In any event — and for whatever reason early humans "broke the ancient primate habit of vegetarianism"[26] — in the light of what is known about comparative physiology, and about early societies, the widely held assumptions about our origins as primitive hunters and flesh-eaters are now questioned. From teeth, jaws and saliva right through the alimentary canal, our bodies are very different from those of the carnivores. We loosely call ourselves omnivorous, but that is through our own choice, not design. Actually our bodies most closely resemble the frugivorous apes and we are very different indeed from nature's true omnivores who eat flesh, carrion and plants. After digestion in the intestines of humans, meat becomes infested with putrefactive bacteria in the bowel; carnivores have a short and smooth bowel for quick release of toxic wastes, unlike our own longer bowel. Healthy vegetarian mammals have much less noxious excretions than those of the carnivores!

(ii) Health Hazards of Meat

Meat-eating nations have enormous health problems, with the so-called "degenerative" diseases" and "diseases of affluence" caused by accumulations of wastes our bodies can't deal with, reaching epidemic proportions. Many studies have linked cancer with a diet high in animal foods; in 1991 the largest survey of the link between diet and cancer was launched in Europe, and the Imperial Cancer Research Fund is predicting that this will confirm that a diet rich in fruit and vegetables will reduce the risk of cancer, whilst consumption of dairy and animal products will be shown to be a risk factor.

Some of the most recent evidence of meat as a cause of cancer comes from work done by researchers at the Lawrence Livermore National laboratory in California (reported in *New Scientist*, 20 March 1993). Scientists have been able to adapt an accelerator mass spectrometer, normally used by geochemists and archeologists to date rocks, in order to measure the genetic damage done by chemicals at very low concentrations. Thus they have been able to measure the effect of the powerful animal carcinogen methylimidazoquinoxaline as it binds to the cells' DNA material and causes lesions, which are the beginnings of most mutations and tumours. Methylimidazoquinoxaline is formed in tiny amounts during the cooking of meat; this new research shows that its effect is potent in much smaller amounts than had previously been measurable.

There is in fact no real *need* for meat in our diet but it is now certain that there is a very real need for fruit and vegetables. These are prime sources of vitamins C, E and beta-carotene (converted in our bodies to vitamin A), which are the core of a vital group of protective substances called antioxidants. Antioxidants are thought to protect against many diseases including heart disease and cancers, by deactivating the highly toxic by-products of body chemistry known as free radicals.

Other dangers of over-consumption of animal based protein have been suspected for decades, though such unwelcome knowledge has been slow to filter through. But by now, with the high meat consumption in post-war Britain, it is becoming obvious that we are getting something very wrong. The miraculous cleansing powers of our livers help to deal with the poisonous substances formed in the intestines of meat-eaters (skatole, indole, tryamine, phenylethylamine and deoxycholic acid) and an active life in the fresh air helps too, but by the time we reach middle age most people are suffering to varying degrees from some chronic ailment.

Obviously many more factors than diet affect our health, and the quality of food in terms of soil fertility, chemical pollution and factory processing is very important as well as the type of diet itself; but I am certain that animal products per se, however wholesome or "organic" the diet in which they are included, have a deleterious effect on the human system.

The risk of bacterial infections alone is enough to make meat a highly suspect food. As soon as an animal's death occurs, putrefaction begins, and meat is by definition bound to be in some stage of decay, arrested temporarily by freezing, cooking or whatever. Therefore meat as such is more akin to the carrion that nature's scavengers eat than to the fresh food of the hunting animals which is always eaten immediately. Bacteria dangerous to humans, such as Salmonella, are not found only in "contaminated" meat but are among the natural inhabitants of dead flesh. No wonder that official figures show a steady rise in reported cases of food poisoning, as the bacteria become more resistant to our immune systems and our manufactured antibiotics.

Modern farming methods, in fact, have the potential for making meat an even more dangerous food. Disease spreads rapidly when animals are closely packed together, so as a precautionary measure the farmer will give antibiotics to a whole herd when only one animal is infected. Drugs are fed to intensively reared pigs from birth to slaughter. This situation has led to the appearance of "super bugs" — bacteria which can withstand antibiotics. So food poisoning is a much more serious public health threat than it was a generation ago. Meat accounts for 80% of food poisoning, and dairy products for most of the rest. 1991 preliminary results of a study carried out by the research section of the Vegetarian Society confirm that vegetarians carry fewer antibiotic-resistant bacteria than do meat eaters.

Even in what would be normal conditions, only careful

cooking and preserving can prevent bacteria from entering our systems live, since we lack the adaptations of the carnivores to deal with them, such as the shorter bowel and the ten times greater secretions of hydrochloric acid in the stomach. A substance which can so quickly become actually harmful to us, and which needs such careful treatment, can hardly be considered our "natural" food. And when a high meat intake is combined with factory processed and denatured foods, as with, for instance, the Innuit peoples of the Arctic region, the results can be disastrous.[27]

The high concentrations of protein and fat in a diet based on meat are thought to be among the main causes of our modern "diseases of affluence". This is hardly surprising, since the stock raised on our farms is fattened for the meat wholesaler. Meat-eaters are not eating healthy animals, but "pathologically fat-loaded beasts" (Dr Alex Comfort's words). Fat surrounds each muscle and fibre and is put there in the special "finishing" process of overfeeding prior to slaughter in order to obtain the best price for the beast (around £2.00 per kg "deadweight" at the time of writing).

A wild warthog would have perhaps one or two per cent body fat, whereas a farm pig, deprived of any significant amount of exercise, has 40 to 50 per cent body fat. As Dr Vernon Coleman has said in one of his popular newspaper articles, "You would need an electron microscope and the hands of a micro-surgeon to cut the fat out of your steak or Sunday joint".

The animals have, moreover, almost certainly received large doses of antibiotics (and hormones in the case of imported meat) which are passed on to the consumer. It is hardly surprising that our health service is so over-strained.

The 1986 report of the BMA's Board of Science and Education states that "vegetarians have lower rates of obesity, coronary heart disease, high blood pressure, large bowel disorders and cancers and gallstones". Many other studies now confirm the health risks of a meat based diet; the largest survey ever undertaken into the links between diet and health is the first report of the Chinese and American teams, published in 1990/91. This study found that some "degenerative" diseases, particularly heart disease and some forms of cancer, are largely unheard of amongst vegetarian populations.[28]

(iii) Health Hazards of Milk

Our high consumption of milk (Britain consumes more milk than any other European nation) is another of the national habits which has had a noticeably harmful effect on our health. If our bodies are demonstrably not perfectly adapted to meat consumption, they are far less well adapted to drinking the milk of another species, an aberrant activity when you come to think about it. Milk is an infant food and humans are the only adult animal (apart from the *domestic* cat) to take it. Milk, like blood, is a substance which in nature is kept entirely inside the body, being transferred in airtight conditions from mother to infant. Outside the body it is subject to immediate decay and contamination, as with meat, so that extreme processes like pasteurisation have to be employed to keep it "safe".[29] Properly speaking, an animal's milk should not really be seen, let alone sold in bottles by the million.

After infancy, our bodies no longer manufacture the enzymes necessary to digest milk sugar (lactose) and in fact the majority of the world's population, who have not been weaned onto cow's milk, actually cannot tolerate it. "Four reports suggest that 20%–40% of patients aged 5–17 years with repeated abdominal pains in childhood suffered from lactose intolerance, which can often be relieved by excluding dairy milk and derivatives from the diet."[30] Childhood milk allergy is commonly known by parents of young children and eliminating milk from the diet is the first and simplest remedy for many eczema sufferers both adult and infant. Even Cow & Gate admit in their promotional literature for infant foods that one in twenty Europeans cannot tolerate milk, and have predictably developed a soya "milk" to fill this gap in their market.

It seems that the evidence against milk continues to mount. A recent report [31] now links cows' milk with juvenile diabetes. Apparently a protein in the milk interferes with insulin production. But incredibly, the medics who have made the link, instead of discouraging the feeding of cows' milk to infants, are now working on a vaccine!

As well as the so-called "allergies" to cow's milk, which appear as eczema, asthma and all sorts of catarrhal conditions, it is now quite clear that there is a link between high milk consumption and heart disease. The falling death rate from heart disease in Switzerland, for instance — and the story is the same in other European countries — parallels the drop in milk consumption by nearly a half between 1951 and 1976.[32] Children in Europe and the US are found to have alarmingly high levels of blood cholesterol, and this is directly linked with over-consumption of saturated fats, a large proportion of which they take as milk. When asked for his view on heart disease prevention, Sir Douglas Black, then President of the British Medical Association, is quoted in *The Times* of 12 June 1984 as saying "Milk is a major killer. It is nonsense to give it to children in schools".

The health hazards of milk have now become widely known and the industry has had to survive by promoting skimmed milk — an even more unnatural product, when you come to think about it. Milk undoubtedly carries traces of drugs and chemicals used by the farmers; and concentrations of stored poisons increase dramatically up the food chain, so that milk contains much higher levels of environmental pollutants (dieldrin, fluorides, strontium 90) than are found in vegetables.

Far from being our "natural" food, milk has been consumed by humans only in certain civilisations and only in comparatively recent times on an evolutionary timescale (6,000 to 8,000 years); purely dairy herds were not developed in this country until the late 19th century. It is a great pity that our infant reliance on the perfect food has become distorted in adulthood to an addiction to such an unnatural and potentially harmful product. I use the word "addiction" because what babies are weaned on plays a very large part in forming dietary habits; and because the use of milk is tied in with our favourite drugs, tea and coffee (for which the dairy industry must be highly gratified).

There are many other ways of getting the nutrients that we need (and even other ways of whitening our tea). A varied vegan diet can richly provide them. After being vegan for some time, one does not worry in the slightest about whether one is getting adequate amounts of this or that nutrient, and I have found that, given freshness and variety, a non-animal diet is abundantly healthy, even and especially during its severest test, pregnancy and lactation.

(iv) The Protein Myth

People commonly think of animal foods as their source of protein, and are encouraged in this on all sides, from domestic science lessons in schools to the cookery sections in magazines. Indeed, "protein" to most British people automatically means meat, fish, cheese and eggs. There is no link in their minds between protein and cereals, pulses and vegetables — a complete blind spot, as if vegetables actually did *not* contain protein. People subscribe to the myth, perhaps, without even knowing what this magical substance is.

Proteins are amino acids — compounds of nitrogen and other elements which are the building blocks of all plant and animal material. Bread and cereals supply as much protein in the average English diet as does meat,[33] and in a form which the kidneys can cope with better than the concentrated animal proteins. The question is one of the amounts and proportions of the nitrogenous compounds.

Grains and seeds are good sources of protein but have low proportions of two of the amino acids essential to humans; legumes (peas and beans) have a high percentage of these two, whilst being low in two others supplied by grains. Therefore, eating foods from both groups supplies a balance; and research has now shown that the two need not be combined actually at the same meal.[34] If bread were eaten alone, the excess amino acids would not be wasted but would be burned up as energy. Meat, soya and milk are foods which contain the amino acids in good proportions, but the old notion of meat as first-class protein is now generally discarded. Soya products and many nuts are actually better sources of protein.

This combination of grains and beans reflects the traditional food staples of many cultures past and present; for instance, Indian rice and dhal, Mexican corn and beans, American peanut-butter sandwich (peanuts are in fact a legume) . . . and the combination also, of course, reflects traditional patterns of agriculture. Crop rotation including legumes is recognised to be required for healthy farming. What is good for the Earth is, naturally, good for us too.

In the fifties and sixties in Europe and the US, scientists and marketeers elevated protein in the form of meat, fish and eggs almost to an elixir. Factory farming grew up on this myth, along with "science" books that a whole generation of schoolchildren studied — books which virtually ignored the possibility that vegetables and grain might also be adequate sources of protein. At present, the protein myth is in decline (meat advertising has had to concentrate on minerals) though many schools still teach children wrongly on the subject of dietary protein. We are now officially told to obtain calories mainly from complex carbohydrates — grains, potatoes and pulses — which are also good sources of protein. Official recommendations on the percentage of protein in the diet have been revised downwards over the past couple of decades and now stand at about 10%. Pulses are 27% protein, nuts and seeds 13% and grains 12%, so it is easy to see why it is unlikely that a generous grain and pulse-based diet would be deficient in protein.

Individual requirements vary enormously, but 50 gms of protein is an average daily recommendation for an adult; this will certainly be supplied in abundance on a grain, pulse and vegetable-based diet where enough calories are consumed — that is, where a healthy appetite is satisfied.

As a vegan, you will not have to rack your brains or worry about providing elements of the two plant groups (seeds and legumes) in your diet but will automatically find they are there (beans on toast, stew and dumplings, etc). With growing infants and children, slightly more care must be taken when they are too small to cope with the extra bulk often required in a vegan diet. Here, proprietary soya milks are useful, as are nut milks and creams which can be made at home (ground nuts blended into water). Tofu is also good for little ones, with its high protein and calcium content. Obviously, breast milk is the only proper food for babies, and incidentally human milk has less protein than cow's milk. The greater bulk and fibrous nature of a healthy vegan diet mean that the diseases associated with the lack of fibre in an animal-based diet, from constipation to cancer of the bowel, can be avoided.

It is a great tragedy for all the middle-aged and over-weight people in Britain (who have wrongly been led to believe that carbohydrates cause obesity whereas animal protein is the stuff of life) that the protein myth has only recently started to shatter.

One small symptom of the change in emphasis which is now taking place was a diet sheet issued through the Sports Council to Olympic athletes in January 1983. This stressed that complex unrefined carbohydrates should replace concentrated animal proteins because they would provide better quality, energy and endurance in the athletes. "Fresh fruit and vegetables increase the potential of the cells and improve the way the oxygen is used."[35] "Carbo-loading" has now replaced the plate of steak as the pre-match meal and we have many healthy vegan athletes, such as Carl Lewis the world champion sprinter, who testify that animal protein is not needed in the diet at all for first-class health and fitness.

(v) Other Nutrients

VITAMIN B12
Many years ago, someone whom I respected told me that B12 was "the animal vitamin" and without it we would die. Given this terrifying information, I concluded that vegans must be mad and I didn't explore the subject further at that time. The whole complex story of the vitamin is by no means fully understood yet, though it is true that it is essential to our bodies. It is involved with the working of our nervous system and blood formation, and the consequences of its deficiency in our bodies are dire. However, deficiency is related more to other nutritional factors than to our actual intake of the vitamin, and is in fact more common amongst meateaters with a low intake of the folic acid needed for its absorption, than amongst vegans. But because B12 deficiency causes serious health problems, vegans should know about it.

The vitamin is manufactured by micro-organisms such as yeasts and bacteria, and is found in vegetables only rarely, when they have been "contaminated" by those organisms. It is found in plants only where microbes in the soil manufacture it and the plant takes it up (eg comfrey growing in rich soil, and seaweed growing near sewage effluent). As always, the quality of the soil is vitally linked with the quality of the food. Earthworm casts are rich in B12 (as are all animal excreta) and it can possibly be taken up by vegetables under certain conditions. But we cannot rely on organic vegetables if we want to guarantee an intake of the vitamin; we must use a yeast extract or another fortified food. The vitamin used commercially is produced by bacteria growing on vegetable matter.

It is possible that humans have the ability to synthesise the vitamin in our own intestines and that this ability has been diminished by our turning to an omnivorous diet and thereby changing the bacterial content of our gut. Certainly, the constant dosing of ourselves with chlorine through our drinking water will not help the functioning of the micro-organisms which inhabit our intestines, and civilised "hygiene" prevents the accidental intake of some bacteria from the environment. The early vegans who had never heard of B12 may have developed, or redeveloped, the ability to use the B12 produced by micro-organisms in the intestines. Studies have shown that the body's ability to absorb the vitamin increases as its intake diminishes.[36] With so many variables and unknown factors, individuals may vary greatly in their need to have a dietary source, so an intake of about 2 micrograms daily is a good insurance policy. This can be found in fermented food such as tempeh, miso and shoyu, in yeast extracts, in various fortified foods (check the label) or in tablet form. Personally, I have only bothered with a B12 tablet supplement whilst breast feeding. It seems that B12 stored in our liver (where it is stored for years, new vegans take note) is not transferred to the breast milk — and deficiency in infants could cause irreversible and serious problems.

VITAMIN D

Another nutrient of particular interest to vegans is vitamin D. This we manufacture ourselves from sunlight on the skin, but if we lived in darkness our food source might be eggs, dairy produce and fish oil. Luckily the vitamin can be manufactured artificially by irradiating vegetable oil and it is a compulsory component of all margarine, so vegans need not worry about this — again, there is a non-animal source of the nutrient. It is essential for its involvement in the absorption of calcium and phosphorous to form teeth and bones. Vegan margarines are now widely available but of course sunlight remains the main source of the vitamin for vegans and non-vegans alike. Bright sunshine is not necessary (or even safe these days) and simple daylight on the face and forearms will stimulate the formation of the vitamin. A dietary intake would not be necessary for someone leading a healthy outdoor life.

Before 1912, nothing definite was known about vitamins at all and in our own time research is still going on.

CALCIUM

It is worth mentioning this mineral to counteract the misleading information put about in dairy advertising. Calcium is the most abundant mineral in the body and is also found in dark green vegetables, tofu (which has four times the calcium of whole cow's milk), seeds, grains and nuts. Calcium deficiency as such is practically unknown, the main deficiency leading to bone problems being that of vitamin D. Furthermore, it is now known that when intake of animal protein (such as dairy produce!) is high, calcium is actually lost from the body in the urine.[37] Osteoporosis is more common in populations with a high intake of animal protein and is less common amongst vegetarian women over 50 than amongst their omnivorous sisters. The American Dairy Council has spent a fortune trying to prove otherwise, but could not, despite an enormous research effort.[38]

Milk is supposed to be high in calcium, but sunflower seeds contain as much, kale twice as much and sesame seeds 11 times the amount. Half a pint of milk provides 350mg of calcium, whilst one serving of spinach provides 540mg. A varied vegan diet, including the foods mentioned above, would certainly not lack calcium.

IRON

This is another mineral which has received attention in advertising, this time from the Meat and Livestock Commission, who would have us believe that we need meat to provide us with iron. But even meat-eaters get only about one-fifth of their iron from meat. The high vitamin C content of a healthy vegan diet assists in the absorption of iron so that vegans get more than their daily requirements from nuts, pulses, grains and seeds. One advertisement for meat states that "a lean 6oz steak contains about a third of your recommended daily intake" but does not of course mention that this amount can also be supplied by a mere 1oz of pistachio nuts, 3.5oz of spinach or 5.5oz of wholemeal bread.

FATS

There has been much publicity in recent years about the dangers of saturated fats (mostly animal fats) but we do need to know that there is a bodily requirement for fats. We should take about one third of our energy requirement as fat (more for infants) but of this only about 10-15% should be saturated fat. Most common vegetable cooking oils and fats contain a proportion of both types, and the ones that are best for us are sunflower, corn, soya, rapeseed and olive oils.

Vegans, like everyone else, should be aware of the "hidden fats" in processed foods, cakes and biscuits, but do not really need to worry about their blood cholesterol levels unless they have a hereditary problem.

Because fish oils have been promoted recently as a panacea for people who have ruined their health by overconsumption of animal fats, it should be stated that they do not in fact contain fatty acids that have been proved to be essential. According to the 1991 COMA report,[39] the essential fatty acids are linoleic acid — found in most vegetable oils — and alpha linolenic acid, which is found in soya, rapeseed, walnut and linseed oils, leafy vegetables and whole wheat products. So we can dispense with that excuse for fish in the diet. As with all nutrients, fat should not be a problem in a varied vegan diet and in fact vegans are the only group in the population who consistently follow official recommendations on fat intake.

DAILY REQUIREMENTS

I do not find it helpful to discuss recommended daily doses of vitamins etc (RNIs as they are now apparently called — Reference Nutrient Intake, as opposed to the former Recommended Daily Amounts) because with a healthy awareness of food the diet will naturally balance itself. However, it may be helpful to new vegans as a guideline to try to eat foods from the following groups each day:

1. Cereals — in wholemeal bread, rice, oats, millet, rye, pasta
2. Pulses (beans), nuts, seeds
3. Fresh Fruit
4. Dried Fruit — dates, apricots, raisins etc.
5. Salads and vegetables, especially green, orange and red colours

6. Soya products — milk, flour, tofu, TVP etc.
7. Oils and fats
8. Potatoes — alternating with cereals
9. Yeast extracts or fermented products, eg tempeh, miso

Do not worry if you occasionally miss out! Our bodies have a miraculous way of increasing absorption of nutrients that are in short supply. The main thing is to satisfy your appetite whilst eating from all the groups. A nutrient chart is included at the end of the book, but as long as you have a *varied* diet and include a generous proportion of fresh and raw foods, you need hardly bother with it. Needless to say, if you are pregnant or breast feeding you should perhaps make a closer study of the subject and have probably done so already (see Bibliography).

It is gratifying to note that the 1983 NACNE (National Advisory Council on Nutrition Education) report, which still forms the basis of nutritional advice given by professionals, largely confirms what vegans have been saying for years. The seven major recommendations are:

1. Decrease total fat intake — reduce from the national average of 40% of energy intake, to 30%
2. Decrease intake of saturated fats
3. Increase the ratio of polyunsaturated fats
4. Reduce sugar consumption (from the average)
5. Reduce salt consumption (from the average)
6. Increase fibre intake to around 30g per day
7. To compensate for the reduction in fat, increase intake of complex carbohydrates

So someone moving from a "normal" diet to a vegan one would necessarily be fulfilling immediately five out of seven of these requirements.

Regarding nutrition needs not mentioned here, such as the many other vitamins and minerals, you can see even from orthodox food and cookery books that they are easily supplied by the plant kingdom. Do not skimp on iron-rich foods and remember especially the value of green leaves, the darker the better. Photosynthesis is the most important process on Earth and chlorophyll always appears in conjunction with various vital minerals. The beautiful colours of a nicely presented and well balanced vegan meal will always include dark green.

(vi) Why (Strictly) Vegan

Most vegans are healthy people who have taken the trouble to educate themselves about nutrition, and follow the way of life without necessarily giving much thought to it. But so strong is the meat and milk myth in our culture that new vegans often spend an initial period in a frenzy to guarantee themselves the "correct" amounts of nutrients. This springs from the reactionary thinking that the vegan diet is one that is "lacking" rather than one that is in fact wholesome, nutritious and varied in its own right. As a vegan, you won't be "making do" without animal products, but rather you will no longer regard them as food at all, and never think of them in connection with eating.

This might seem very "strict" to someone who has not yet adopted a vegan diet, but, speaking personally, once I had made the decision to do without animal food I felt a sense of exhilaration and release from the cycle of exploitation and suffering. It was a life-enhancing decision, and looking back on it now it was more like a liberation than an act of self-discipline. The reason why vegans are careful where possible to see that they never take animal products is not because of a sanctimonious attitude of wishing to keep their moral integrity untainted (though when I was omnivorous my suspicion of that in vegetarians used to put me off them), but it is partly because we think it important to illustrate to others that good health can be maintained entirely without animal products.

To indulge even occasionally in milk or eggs, apart from helping to support an industry that we hope to close down, might undermine the case for pure vegetarianism. It is also true that after a period of true vegetarianism, meat and milk begin to seem horrifying and pathetic substances — certainly not things one would wish to consume unless severely pressed. Vegans are still pioneers in the sense that we have to show everyone else that our common sense viewpoint and diet also encourage happiness and good health.

On the other hand, flag-waving can be a little off-putting, too. But it is necessary at times, since the eating habits of the rich world will probably have to change if we are to survive, either in economic terms or as healthy people. Vegans are still unfortunately a tiny minority and the forces involved in maintaining the food markets are enormous, as we have seen. From the nutritional angle alone, the vegan case is clear. The biggest threats to world health are malnutrition in the Third World, and degenerative disease in the West (both social and economic, not medical, problems). These extremes are aggravated by animal farming, which must be wound down before true and lasting social progress will be made.

CHAPTER SIX

ANIMAL EXPLOITATION

"I am a vegetarian for the same reason that I am not a cannibal" — Brigid Brophy

Supported by the facts of economics and nutrition, veganism is a mattter of basic common sense. Despite its unfortunate eccentric or hypermoralistic overtones, veganism per se is not a religion, though all of the world's great religions have had an element of vegetarianism. Simple compassion is what turns most people to veganism.

(i) The Realities of Slaughter

By eating meat, eggs and dairy products, we base our lives on killing. Film footage shown on national television news recently has shown that the animals' journey to slaughter can be long and cruel, and that slaughterhouses themselves are terrifying places, where animals can die of fright before they reach the slaughter pens. "A 'shot' lamb is one that has panicked at the slaughterhouse in the moments before it dies . . . its systems have burst with fright and it is virtually inedible."[40] Farmers well know, too, that pigs can die of fright and so will feed them vitamin E to try to avoid heart attack prior to slaughter — a cruel irony. On the other hand, "Killing at a moment of fear creates a chemical process which lessens the growth of bacteria during curing".[41] Evidently a fine balance of terror is necessary.

The infamous 1984 official report of the Farm Animal Welfare Council destroyed the myth that animals are slaughtered humanely, and made horrifying reading. Even though the inspecting Council members always announced their visits, unnecessary cruelty was found at every stage of the proceedings, from unloading to actual slaughter, for which the animals were often fully conscious. The slaughtermen in most of our 800 or so abattoirs are on piece rates; compassionate techniques can hardly be followed at high speed and so the stunning bolt or electric tongs are often carelessly used; the animal is then strung up by a hind leg to have his or her throat cut whilst still conscious.

The animal is normally alive for up to ten minutes after the throat is cut so that the heart beat and breathing will drain the blood from the meat. This gives the animal plenty of time to regain consciousness before the moment of death, if stunning has not been carried out correctly. During all this, even existing legislation is not being followed, so it is unlikely that future legislation would lead to an improvement in procedures. Recent improvements following bad publicity, and the imminent closure of half of our abattoirs, are on hygienic rather than humanitarian grounds.

In spite of what people would like to believe about "dumb" animals, they have a perfectly developed nervous system and, faced with the prospect of slaughter, reactions similar to our own. Though our abattoirs are more secret that our crematoria and our prisons, and though we may try to forget, by concealing them, the millions of suffering creatures that we sacrifice each year to the meat and milk myth, somewhere in our subconscious or our nightmares we must know that it is "Belsen every day" for the animals. This is the basis of any diet which is not vegan.

(ii) Conditions on Farms

It is not necessary to dwell on the evils of factory farming in order to make a case for veganism, but it is very relevant today when farm management is dictated by the company accountant rather than the stockman. Simply to stay in business, farmers must extract the greatest possible "yield" from their animals. "Unfortunately it is advantageous to stock above the recommended rates because the increased throughput more than compensates for increased mortality."[42] (There is also a huge social cost in factory farming, which has worsened the depopulation of our countryside and increased the overcrowding of our cities.)

In the case of the prolific pig (a modern unit of 100 sows can produce 2,500 piglets a year) the "increased through-put" means injecting piglets with chemical growth boosters to reach their slaughter weight in just 22 weeks; tranquillisers are also used to subdue pigs kept in overcrowded stalls; and the normal practice of keeping the breeding sows tethered and completely immobilised by iron bars will not become illegal in the UK until 1998.

The main problem with factory farming is that by extreme feeding and breeding procedures, the animals are forced to grow so quickly that an enormous strain is placed on their systems. A pig at slaughter weight will often have heart disease, and legs and hips too weak to bear her own weight; and a 35-day old broiler bird (who will be allowed to "live" until about 22 days) is too weak to stand. (A typical broiler unit will contain a quarter of a million birds.)

Even fish are not exempt from these procedures, and intensive fish farming is now very big business. In salmon farming, fish who would by nature migrate across oceans, are kept at a stocking level of 15kg of fish per cubic metre of water. They, too are fed high-protein pellets containing antibiotics. Several weeks before slaughter they are starved, because it is less messy to gut a starved fish. There is a 20% mortality rate, and many swimming fish have skin ulcerations and tumours.[43]

So the life of most farm animals is horrific even before the horrors of slaughter.

Firstly, the sheer callousness with which animals are treated during "husbandry" (the meaning of the word derives entirely from economics) which assumes that they exist merely to be used in a similar way to machines, has little regard for welfare. An amazing 16,000 large animals die unnecessarily each day (yes, sixteen thousand each day) on British farms.[44] This is through exposure, starvation, drug side-effects or sheer neglect, and this fact alone is sufficient indictment of most farmers. If young ones are said to die from "maternal" neglect, rather than the farmer's neglect, then that is because the farmer's inbreeding has neglected maternal qualities in favour of qualities of flesh or wool, etc. I recently mentioned mortality rates to a farmer, and he said "Sheep don't WANT to live"! And neither would I, if I were "owned" by him.

Farming accounts for many more animal deaths by accident than vivisection does by design (in recent years vivisection has claimed approximately 3 million animal lives per year). Veterinary supervision is not required by law in treatment of farm animals despite the massive reliance by farmers on medication, so that most vets these days make their livings from the more profitable household pets industry.

I have often heard the cry: "But I love animals! I grew up on a farm/in the country!" What kind of "love" is it that would rear a creature for slaughter? Farmers talk about their favourite animals with the same kind of "love" with which some people talk about their cars. A farm is the last place on Earth where a true animal lover would feel at home.

It will now be useful to explain why a "vegetarian" is just as much involved with slaughter as is an omnivore.

(iii) The Dairy Cow

Despite what the dairy industry would have us believe, with its insulting advertising, cow's milk is NOT a necessary food for humans nor is it a natural gift from the cow. As with all mammals, including ourselves, a cow produces milk only after giving birth, for the purpose of feeding her young. Every dairy cow is made pregnant each year by artificial insemination (or embryo transplant for the wealthy farmer) and the pregnancy, like our own, lasts for nine months. For six to seven months each year she is milked whilst pregnant.

On giving birth her calf is removed after only a few hours — if it were left with her there would be very little milk left for humans. After this separation she mourns for her calf for many days — the distressed braying of cows is a familiar sound in the countryside. Most calves go to market to be sold later as veal, after a miserably short motherless existence (in this respect, lambs and beef herds have a much better life).

When the calf is taken away, the cow will be attached to mechanical pumps twice a day to encourage and maintain her milk supply — obviously a calf would suckle more frequently than this. Any female will understand that the tenderest spots are touched, or rather brutalised, here. To encourage lactation when the offspring is dead seems to me most repugnant, adding insult upon injury. To maintain unnaturally high yields of milk, the cow will be fed on concentrated protein pellets rather than her natural diet of grass. The problem of slurry pollution has already been noted:

"The diets we give cattle mean they end up with
permanent diarrhoea" [45]

This digestion problem causes the cow to have acidosis of
the rumen, leading to the severe pain and lameness of
laminitis, as well as causing the other common disease
mastitis, though debilitation and poor hygiene.

(iv) BSE

The unnatural diet is also responsible for a potential catastrophe, lightheartedly named "mad cow disease". This is
Bovine Spongiform Encephalopathy (BSE), a fatal and
incurable disease related to Scrapie in sheep and Creutzfeldt-
Jakob Disease in humans; the efffect is disintegration of the
brain. The chemistry of the agent causing the infection is
still not known at the time of writing, though there are
instances of its transmission between species. The point is
that its occurrence in cattle was found to be the result of
feeding to the cattle, in those concentrated protein pellets,
the remains of sheep infected with Scrapie. This feed would
have come from a "rendering plant" — a factory dealing with
the remains of slaughtered animals, which are added to
animal feeds and described as "concentrates", protein sup-
plements or bone meal. Through this process we were
feeding cows to cows and forcing the gentle herbivores into
cannibalism.

After this new disease hit the headlines in Britain,
government measures were taken in an effort to prevent a
massive scare, but they were taken far too late. In 1988,
100% compensation for infected animals was announced,
whereupon reported cases immediately doubled — an illus-
tration that farmers were previously passing off infected
animals through the market. In any case, symptoms of the
disease appear long after its onset, so that it is impossible to
stop infected animals from entering the food chain. Current

regulations which dictate the removal of "high risk" organs from slaughtered animals may or may not be effective since it is simply not known where in the animal's body the infecting agent is located.

Professor Richard Lacey of Leeds University Department of Microbiology has warned that we could be in for "a crisis of major proportions" and in 1992 the infection rate in cattle is still rising at a rate far higher than predicted by government experts as we sit back and wait for its incubation period in humans to be completed. It has already been demonstrated that the disease can be transferred experimentally, since a patient in a British hospital contracted Creutzfeldt-Jakob Disease when bovine membranes infected with BSE were grafted routinely into the patient's brain during an operation.[46] And now, two dairy farmers have died from C-J-D.[47]

Meanwhile, dairy cows are still being fed on unnaturally high concentrations of protein and there is still no legal compulsion to label the ingredients of animal feed though of course the public has been reassured that everything is under control. (And though there is now a supposed ban on animal protein in cattle feed, this is not extended to pigs and poultry.)

By means of this unnatural diet, and also by genetic control and lack of exercise, the cow's milk yield has been grotesquely multiplied, as we have already seen. Bovine Somatotropin (BST), the artificial hormone secretly tested on 15 farms in the UK, aims to increase the yield even further by 20%.[48] This terrific strain on her system leads to a disease-prone existence. A Ministry survey estimated that over one third of cows suffer from mastitis, the agonisingly painful breast infection, despite regular injections of penicillin through the teats; this is not surprising when distended udders are close to a filthy floor in confined conditions. And there is a 25–30% rate of laminitis.[49] In fact, a dairy cow's udder is so prolapsed towards the end of her life that a calf could not suckle in its natural position anyway. No wonder that she is prematurely exhausted after only four lactations, when her natural life span would be at least 20 years. "The ideal approach is to breed from the cow as early as is practical and take two to three calves. . . . It should then be slaughtered before it reaches mature size."[50]

All this, to produce a product which is in surplus! People generally think that milk comes in bottles, and they think no further. In reality, each pinta represents a quantity of discomfort and distress — stockpiling or wasting the product, mountains of suffering.

The calves are a lucrative by-product of the dairy industry and have a pitiful journey from the dairy farm to their horrific destination. Many are exported to the notorious veal crates which are now banned in the UK. Many will be slaughtered very young, since the insides of their stomachs are needed for the rennet in cheese-making. So-called "vegetarian" cheese which uses different enzymes conveniently overlooks the fact that the calves have to die anyway if we are to have a dairy industry. Vegetarians who drink milk are in fact helping to worsen the plight of the modern dairy cow, who goes to slaughter prematurely exhausted, and is one of the most intensively expoited and insensitively treated animals of all times. Life in a vivisection laboratory might be comparatively pleasant.

Our cattle are not truly indigenous and are certainly not a natural part of our landscape, the familiar breeds we now know having been developed in the 19th century and later. For pity's sake, would not extinction be better for them.

(v) Egg Production

There is no end to human ingenuity in devising maximum profit from manipulating other species, and there is no species of farm animal that has not undergone generations of genetic manipulation. The poor things are all freaks. And the situation will become far worse for them when the potential horrors of genetic engineering (transferring characteristics between species) are unfolded.

For those who eat eggs, modern technology has brought us the battery hen — condemned to a life sentence in her torturously overcrowded cage until she dies of exhaustion or cannibalism, her uterus grossly prolapsed through the relentless laying induced on her, and never to see anything except the suffering and death of her own kind in a 17-hour daily cycle of artificial light (to counteract an autumn decline in production.) But natural instincts are still present and it would be arrogant to assume that, never having known anything else, the hen will be "happy" in this environment. This is illustrated by the speed with which a liberated battery hen will return to a more natural condition and start activities like scratching, bathing in earth, and perching, which she has never been allowed and which many generations of her family have not ever seen.

A modern-day hen will live in a unit of 50,000 or so birds (merely several thousand in the case of a "free range" unit) and she will lay 300 eggs per year. 10% of the hen's normal calcium reserves are used in each egg.[51] Despite massive unnatural feeding, this calcium depletion leads to osteoporosis in most laying hens and 30% of "spent" hens have broken bones. Commercial laying hens (whether producing "barn" eggs or "fresh" eggs) are only allowed to "live" for one year, and many will die of exhaustion before the year is up.

Even "free range" hens hardly live a natural existence, and here again people have some pretty naive ideas about farmers' wives merely "collecting" the surplus eggs which nature supplies in abundance. The wild counterpart of the domestic hen lays only about half a dozen eggs in a series, possibly only once a year. The absolute maximum would be a dozen eggs per year. She will not usually do this unless she has a mate — unfertilised eggs rarely occur in the wild. Having mated, the fowl will lay an egg daily until she has a comfortable number to sit on. She will then incubate and care for the young. She can lay extra eggs to replace lost ones, but this is regulated by the amount of food required by her.

The colossal number of eggs produced by domestic hens comes about by the eggs being continually removed, and by prodigious feeding, nowadays with protein concentrates, dyestuffs (to colour the yolks) and synthetic hormones being an accepted ingredient of chicken feed. The inevitable result is, of course, exhaustion and early slaughter. Even so-called "free range" hens are not allowed to live after they have stopped producing eggs.

What vegetarian egg eaters tend to forget also is that, like cows, hens produce male offspring in equal numbers to the females. For nearly every laying hen in existence, a male chick has been slaughtered and this of course applies also to free-range flocks of whatever size. The details of this, in modern hatcheries, are not very pleasant. No rules govern their slaughter, since they are not destined for human consumption. After sexing, the unlucky males are sometimes thrown live into a mincer, to convert them into fertiliser or feedstuff for other animals, or sometimes simply thrown into polythene bags to suffocate en masse or to be gassed with carbon dioxide. Often they survive and are noticed moving about amongst dead birds brought to the rendering plant. All this takes place at high speed and with conveyor-belt efficiency as befits huge industries like Cobb and Ross, our main broiler dealers. This is the reality behind the images of fluffy, chirpy yellow chicks (as indeed they are) which are used commercially at Easter time.

(vi) The Myth of the Hunter

Possibly plants, too, have an inscrutable "nervous system" of a kind and in some way "feel" and "suffer".[52] They are after all part of the sensitive fabric of the living Earth. But if you eat animals instead you are of course responsible for the destruction of many more plants than if you ate plants alone. And death is in any case a natural part of the cycle of life — luckily most people who read this will have a degree of choice in which particular food cycle they adopt and whether or not they are responsible for animal deaths.

The numbers of animals suffering on our farms are almost too difficult to imagine. Over six hundred million farm animals are slaughtered each year;[53] 4,000 animals every minute of every working day.

Not many of us would witness the daily scenes at our slaughterhouses, where comparatively young creatures are dragged and goaded, confused and terrified, away from their kin and into the slaughter pens, without our feeling great horror and equally great compassion. Not many could even watch the actual slaughter, which has to be left to a few case-hardened individuals. Even those rare people who kill their own meat, which seems the much more honest thing to do, usually have to steel themselves to learn the skills of slaughter.

Where, then, does our revulsion come from? The true carnivores kill without compassion (and their quarry is allowed its natural reactions of flight and struggle). Why does slaughter have to be hedged with secrecy and why do some religions still keep their ancient rules and taboos surrounding it, which we in the West have mostly lost (except in respect of a few favoured mammals)? Might we suspect from all this that killing for food is not natural to us?

Though it has become fashionable to admire the hunting rituals of other cultures, which certainly present more to admire than some of the social habits of our own culture, the hunting "instinct" has been much overplayed in recent years and particularly since the film, *The Deer Hunter* (set partly in the States and partly in Vietnam), which probably did more for the game park "hunting" industry in America than for the anti-war effort.

The meat myth, along with the misconceptions in nutrition already mentioned, has produced other misconceptions. One is the "survival of the fittest", taken to mean "the stongest" rather than "the most adaptable to circumstance", i.e. "fit" meaning "suitable". Another is "man the primitive hunter". Hunting is widely supposed to be humankind's original food-finding activity, yet this is not the case, as we have seen. The hunting theme is now tied in somewhere with the human self-image, which is unfortunate and also ironic, since certainly in Britain hunting has never been a vital means of survival throughout the centuries of recorded history. It has been the privilege of the rich and the last resort of the poor.

One hypothetical question which I have often heard put to vegetarians is whether we would hunt and kill for food in an emergency situation; but like many hypothetical arguments this just does not have grounds in reality, and fits no emergency situation which could arise in an industrialised country. A hunting community needs a very wide range of land to provide and sustain its natural prey. I have read that to feed the population of Britain by hunting wild animals, an area more than that of the entire world would be needed. This is why hunting has only ever been a game for the rich in any populous civilisation. What does go back for many years, however, is the domestication of animals, and not only for food.

(vii) Our Other Little (and Big) Captives – Pets

Animals have nervous systems, highly developed like our own, and intelligence suited to their particular ecological niche. They live and breathe as we do, and are in a sense our kin, and there is a residual awareness of this in the minds of those animal lovers who like to keep pets and are concerned with the welfare of animals, whether wild or domestic. Unfortunately the notion that animals exist for our use, or at least that we are justified in using or exploiting them, has rooted itself so deeply in our culture over the centuries that it has perverted this residual awareness into a ghastly parody of kinship with animals — the household pets industry.

Domestic pets have very little chance of living a fulfilled life, in the sense of utilising all the faculties with which nature has equipped them. Every caged bird or rodent, every confined or restrained creature however exotic or mundane, is condemned to a lifetime of deprivation of its natural activities of food-finding, self-preservation and mating, and to solitary confinement from the intricate social structure of which individuals of all species are a part. To say that the "wilder" qualities of our domestic animals and pets have been "bred" out of them and therefore they do not suffer, is simply not true, and this is illustrated for instance by the case of the battery hen already mentioned (p.61). Every pet shop, every hutch, cage or pen, represents a degree of suffering to which our conditioning has made us insensitive. If set free, domestic pets would have no ecological niche and would quickly perish or cause chaos. Our love of animals has put them into a sorry predicament indeed.

Even the dog, or perhaps especially the dog, in our society of so-called animal lovers, suffers endless periods of boredom and frustration for every hour or so that s/he is properly stimulated by work or play. And living in the close confinement of modern-day families, with all the stresses involved, has even produced the neurotic dog, who is either an unfortunate child substitute or simply a sufferer within an unhappy family atmosphere. All this is before considerations of the actual cruelty caused by the keeping of pets. Each time the R.S.P.C.A. releases its annual figures on animal abuse, they are higher; and because we breed dogs indiscriminately either through profit or ignorance, 1,000 unwanted dogs are put down in Britain every working day.[54]

It seems obvious that all living creatures are "designed" for certain lifestyles (only the lifestyle most suited to humankind is most variable and in question). That humans' extreme possessiveness over material things has spilled over to include the weaker species as objects, so that we can actually have the arrogance to say that an animal "belongs" to someone (and this is upheld in law), seems to me a distortion of the natural order. To use the word "design" calls up all sorts of theological questions, but to assume a natural order is surely tenable. Perhaps one day we will reject the notion of "owning" animals, just as we have now rejected the practice of owning humans, i.e. slavery.

Meanwhile, the keeping of pets is part of our culture and in fact in the UK is a £2 billion per year industry. Surely there is something very amiss in our society where we live in overcrowded cities and yet confine animals together with us for "companionship". Animals are pathetically exploited to provide the hugging and stroking which humans need but which is often taboo.

And if we are true animal lovers, we would not wish to be responsible through the food we feed to cats and dogs for maintaining the slaughterhouses, which can cut their losses by selling the least attractive meat to the pet food industry. To keep an omnivorous pet, and to feed it on the dead flesh of other equally sensitive and intelligent creatures, is surely a gross irony. It is possible for dogs to be vegan, now that there is a commercial vegan dog food, but cats are true carnivores and the supplement developed to enable them to be healthy on a vegetable-based diet[55] has hardly had a massive response. Nevertheless I would think that every vegetarian who keeps a cat is duty bound to try it.

It is a mark of our insensitivity and our double standards when the pet food industry in a nation of animal lovers actually props up the meat industry, not to mention encouraging the mass slaughter of such creatures as whales (in the not too far distant past) and kangaroos (in the present). Activist vegetarians who keep cats should be reminded that they are campaigning to end the industry which provides food for their pets.

The relationship between a person and another animal can be a beautiful thing, fraught though it is with human-centred misconceptions like animals being "faithful" and being "good". But with the modern-day "ownership" of cats and dogs, this involves the need for slaughterhouses, an evil which should outweigh all other considerations. In an ideal future there would be no captive pets, but a range of wild and semi-wild animals inhabiting the tracts of land that could be returned to nature under a vegan economy. Only then could we truly recover our community with animals — an impossible dream in the present circumstances. Animals in the countryside are quite sensibly terrified of humans and you have to go to a city park to have a relationship with a squirrel or a bird.

Not all pets, of course, are carnivores. I used to have a dream of establishing a colony of vegetarian animals, a paradigm of peaceful coexistence where guinea-pigs and tortoises would potter about amongst brightly-plumed birds and other decorative creatures, without fear. But apart from the massive importation of grains that this little prison camp would need, healthy breeding animals living outside their natural environment would soon overpopulate their home. There would have to be either a trade to local pet shops, with all the horrifying possibilities that would involve, or a mass sterilisation or isolation programme of the inmates. In my view there is no justification for tampering with other animals and their environment in such ways. My old dream now seems very sentimental indeed.

(viii) Zoos

Zoos are another ancient barbaric institution and not places for real animal lovers. Guy the gorilla (RIP), prisoner and star attraction of one of our most respected zoological institutions (a little tarnished since it was shown to be involved with vivisection), whose whole family group was slaughtered in order to bring him to his new home, used to symbolise the utter hopelessness of the situation of animals like him. Two modern excuses for maintaining zoos (which exist primarily to make money and to further careers) are for their educational role, and for protecting endangered species.

But to observe animals in captivity, even in so-called "safari parks", is only an education in the ways of human insensitivity — for it seems that visitors do not even realise that what they are watching is a cruel and grotesque parody of animal life. Removed from their natural environment with its thousands of ever-present intricate demands — the carnivores deprived even of their deepest psychological need, to catch their food — they can do nothing but sink into inactivity or patterns of repetitive neurotic behaviour. Surely natural history books, and films of animals in the wild, are a far better education in the ways of animals.

As for the conservation aspect, it is certainly more cost-effective in terms of protecting endangered species (i.e. many species, perhaps thousands — not just a few captive specimens) to spend money on preserving wild areas than on breeding animals in zoos. There is already a list of creatures extinct in the wild that exist in zoos, and for which it is virtually impossible to recreate a natural habitat. Protecting our few remaining natural animal habitats must surely now be the most urgent priority.

Space forbids a close look at circuses, which have by now been publicly discredited.[56] But we can welcome the fact that many local Councils have banned from their land circuses which use "performing" animals, recognising that, even if there were no cruelty involved (which there undoubtedly is), watching animals perform unnatural acts is not really an appropriate entertainment for a civilised society. There are now many brilliant and far more entertaining circuses which use only performing humans.

(ix) The Double Standard

If I have dwelt over-long on the issue of other captive animals, it is because I regard it as an aspect of our wrong assumptions which has been overlooked for too long. (Not every vegan would agree with me, of course.) People who use animals as surrogate friends usually eat animals too. They claim affection for animals whilst turning a blind eye to the brutality we inflict upon them. This is a double standard which permeates our society. If a farmer kept a dog permanently tethered in a small pen he would be liable to prosecution under the Protection of Animals Act 1911, yet for doing this to equally intelligent pigs he will receive grant aid. Similarly, poultry are of course excluded from the Protection of Birds Act 1954, which makes it an offence to keep any bird in a cage where it cannot spread its wings. And if you now did to a badger what you are legally allowed to do to a fox, you could well be imprisoned.

Training for acceptance of the double standard starts early, with our nursery songs and children's stories (which provide a fascinating study in anthropomorphism and mixed-up thinking). We encourage our children to be fond of animals and to keep them in boxes, jars and hutches, and we grow up with a spurious love of the countryside, not seeing it for what it really is — a defoliated expanse around the animals' concentration camps.

In fact, insensitivity is the order of the day amongst country dwellers, and this is hardly surprising. I can think of nothing more obnoxious than rearing and protecting animals until near maturity, only to lead them to slaughter. Treachery is too mild a word for this. A society which, as we have seen, bases its existence on killing, must have a degree of insensitivity to violence. Slaughterhouse towns have been observed to have a higher than normal rate of crime.[57] Perhaps the atmosphere of death which hangs over them, and which animals of course can sense, works in subtle ways on the human psyche. That there is such a connection is referred to extensively in literature and is perhaps implicitly understood by most people who have thought about it, but the subject has never to my knowledge been thoroughly explored in a scientific or academic way.

When Upton Sinclair wrote his novel *The Jungle* in 1906, set around the stockyards and slaughterhouses of Chicago, he did not intend to make a case for the animals, but to expose the appalling working and living conditions of the workers — though he does observe: "there seemed to be something about the work of slaughtering that tended to ruthlesness and ferocity" and there is even a passing reference to the fact that the new socialist industrial republic would be vegetarian: "it has been proven that meat is unnecessary as food; and meat is obviously more difficult to produce than vegetable food, less pleasant to prepare and handle, and more likely to be unclean."

So these ideas were around in 1906! Some would say that we have not come very far since then.

(x) Conscientious Consumerism

> "It is also true that a man sees more of things themselves when he sees more of their origin; for their origin is a part of them, and indeed the most important part of them."
> — G.K. Chesterton, *St Francis of Assisi*

Compassion for suffering animals does not begin and end with animals but acknowledges the ultimate unity of all life. Now, in Britain today, a majority of people probably do not know in their hearts that paper is trees, leather is skin, and meat is flesh.[58] But when we start to question what blood has been shed for the food we eat, we also question who has died of hunger whilst grain has been fed to our cattle, who has laboured on plantations or in mills for our food and fabrics, and who has crawled underground to fetch the ore which makes our trinkets, ornaments and nuclear warheads. The list is endless. No single question is really separable from the whole.

No one can be quite free from the cycle of exploitation which keeps the economic system turning over, but by refusing animal products wherever possible — and this is totally possible where food is concerned — we can take a huge step forward out of the morass. Educated people living in the affluent countries often may feel some degree of responsibility for the economic imbalance which supports their relatively luxurious lifestyle, and the guilt thereby created, conscious or subconscious, could be one of the causes of our society's malaise. Giving a minute fraction of our income occasionally to some worthy cause may or may not make much difference, but becoming vegan is a way for us to shed at least some of the guilt, and achieve a substantial lightening of conscience.

Moreover on a rational level, we can free ourselves from the discomfort of maintaining the double standard, where we can on the one hand claim affection for certain fluffy or feathered creatures whilst on the other hand enjoying the harvest of animal agony. Life becomes clearer and more logical. And, more important, by adopting the most ecologically sound diet we can dramatically reduce the amount of devastation of Earth's resources for which we are personally responsible.

> "Nobody made a greater mistake than he who did nothing because he could only do a little"
> — Edmund Burke

There are many highly principled people these days who refuse any Third World product on the grounds that transnational trade automatically, under the present system, works to the disadvantage of the producers of the primary product. There are others who buy only through an organisation like Tradecraft or Equal Exchange (see contacts list), which put profits back into co-operatives and self-help organisations at grass roots level in the developing countries. Whichever path we choose as responsible consumers, by becoming vegan we immediately reduce drastically the gross amount we consume. If we change our consumer habits, then gradually the market economies will change accordingly.

The main obstacle to these changes being widely adopted, however, is not people's illogicality but their indifference. Most people, unfortunately, seem not to be truly concerned about any tragedy which takes place outside the realms of their own home or workplace (nor even about the possibility of a nuclear holocaust or a man-made climatic catastrophe). The millions who live in dire poverty and the quiet victims of stock farming are not particularly high in their consciousness. But I think that change is at least possible. After all, every reform in our society from the abolition of slavery to the opening of public libraries and contraceptive services has had to overcome the fierce resistance of the powerful and the broad indifference of the majority. Our next reform must go literally to the grass roots.

"If you are not part of the solution, you are part of the problem."

CHAPTER SEVEN

MEAT AND WAR

"As long as there are slaughterhouses, there will be battlefields." — Leo Tolstoy

As we have seen, the food we eat has a very high cost in Earth's resources and animal suffering. Fundamentally, it is not "good" for us. Basing our lives on killing creatures who have no defence against us damages both our health and our sensitivity. Our just reward for this callousness towards the rest of creation is not only the prevalence of incurable disease in the affluent countries, but also the constant warfare, which has been a major feature of the history of the West.

(i) The First Wars

As we are more physiologically akin to the frugivorous apes than to any other animal, perhaps once in the past we lived peacefully amongst other creatures, as they do. The mythologies of most cultures have remnants of an awareness of this, and our own is no exception. Though I hesitate to quote from the Bible, where you can find a text to condone almost anything, and many of them contradictory, it is of interest to mention here that amongst the very first instructions given to humans were some about our diet:

> "I give you all plants that bear seed everywhere on
> Earth, and every tree bearing fruit which yields
> seed: they shall be yours for food." — Genesis 1.29

The "permission" to eat flesh which came later, after Noah's flood, was surely a temporary expedient meant only for a period when there was no vegetation. For the prime, unequivocal rule that was never superseded is "Thou shalt not kill". Moreover, the Bible indicates that we should have "dominion" over other species, which points to our duties of conscious stewardship. Many cultures have a collective myth or memory of a long-lost era of peace and harmony with the world. There are many legends of the "garden" which provided our food. Our word "paradise" comes from an ancient Persian word which denoted a walled garden.

It could be that changing environmental conditions made man into a killer (and only flint gave the small-toothed humans the power to eat the food of the lion) but this happened relatively suddenly in evolutionary terms, and so the rituals which the natural carnivores have, to prevent them from killing each other, simply did not evolve. Thus the peculiarly human phenomenon of warfare began.

Or perhaps killing for food made our ancestors more inclined to kill for other reasons. Certainly, ancient history shows a conflict between the peoples of the settled agricultural regions of Southern Europe and the Near East and the more warlike nomads, with their flocks and herds, attacking from the north. (The biblical story of Cain and Abel is a paradigm of this.) It was the need for large areas of land for grazing animals which caused the violent disruption of early patterns of civilisation. I believe that the word "war" comes originally from an ancient Aryan word meaning "desire for more cows".[59] The word "cattle" has the same derivation as "chattel" and "capital". The mobile tribes of herders transformed Europe over a period of 3,000 years from a culture of sustainable agrarian groups to one in which land was something to capture and exploit.[60] And the extreme brutality and treachery of animal slaughter, as meat-eating increased with "progress", could have had a mounting effect on human acceptance of war over the centuries.

It is a sad thought that this conection between meat-eating and violence is even condoned in our society. Along with the meat myth, we have been conditioned into accepting that a certain amount of violence is natural and even necessary. Soldiers and butchers can be popular and esteemed characters, representing the essence of "manhood"; vegetarians and pacifists on the other hand are popularly thought of as weaklings and cowards, unable to face the "facts" of life and a danger to the true grit of the nation. In fact, the history of pacifism is one of strength and bravery, and as for vegetarianism, we now have world-class vegan athletes who belie the popular assumptions.[61]

(ii) Food and International Relations

Since ancient times when men and women first fought for land, the wheel has come full circle. Having destroyed the indigenous cultures of other nations in our rapacious search for more and ever more raw materials, food and fuel to feed the monstrous notion of the expanding economy, rich Western countries are in a position to use food almost as a weapon. At the time of the OPEC assertiveness in the early seventies, the US Secretary for Agriculture spoke of food as a "powerful tool in our negotiating kit", and at the United Nations General Assembly in 1974, President Ford actually threatened the use of food as a weapon against the OPEC countries.

It seems that the pattern of world trade which has developed around the sophisticated lifestyle and diet encouraged in the West has created a situation where the poorer countries, robbed of their self-sufficiency by post-colonial cash crop economics, are the easy victims of the world's most powerful institutions like the World Bank and the IMF. Yet the 1974 World Food Conference maintained that each country should be self-sufficient in food.

We have already seen that the easiest way to self-sufficiency both in temperate and in tropical climates is basing the diet on food which comes directly from the land, that is, not through the bodies of animals. Developing countries would at least have a surer footing if sufficient traditional subsistence crops were allowed to be grown before the crops which supposedly make money on the international market. It would be nice to think that trade encouraged good international relations, but history has shown that this is far from the case. A return to self-sufficiency in food for all nations would be a sound basis for world peace. This is the ultimate aim of veganism.

With this awareness of our vegetarian origins, and the need to return to regional self-sufficiency, it may seem that vegans are more than somewhat retrogressive, possibly having a half-baked wish to go back to the Garden of Eden. This is not so. There is no going back, for we have destroyed a large part of our environment; and in any case growth and change are inherent in all life. We need to move forward with appropriate technology in the massive programme of afforestation which is required in order to help to heal the wounds we have inflicted upon the Earth.

Some degree of self-sufficiency is an ideal which has necessarily been part and parcel of many alternative movements. A regional self-sufficiency, and certainly self-sufficiency of all nations in staple foods, could be the vegan contribution to global political stability. At the local level, at least one UK family of four has shown that it can be self-sufficient in food and fuel on less than four acres of land (details from MCL, see contacts list). This is less than the amount of land that would be arrived at if all the fertile land in Britain were divided equally amongst the present population.

Unfortunately it does not seem that our agricultural land is about to be redistributed. Land reform programmes are outside the scope of this book, but it can be said that we are certainly a long way from a situation of each family having its own plot and producing its own food and fuel. Personally I do not favour this in any case. Community-scale, not family-scale, farming and horticulture seem more appropriate. Not everyone would want to spend a high proportion of time on the land, though there are many worse jobs, and veganic culture could certainly involve far less drudgery than animal farming, particularly in winter. Perhaps the ideal lies somewhere along the lines of Fritz Schumacher's "cantonised system of largely self-sufficient communities" described in his influential book *Small in Beautiful*. For the moment, regional self-sufficiency in staple foods is surely what we should be encouraging our government to aim for, and meanwhile through market forces we can direct the growers to produce what is good for us.

In a vegan future, with the science and skills already acquired, we could inhabit garden cities and villages which would provide food, recreation and creative employment for us all. Afforestation ideals go back at least as far as Plato, who spoke of happier times when Attica's mountains were tree-clad. This is now no pipedream, but something that is recognised to be possible and necessary. If we want to have enough oxygen for our life to continue, we simply cannot afford to transform even more land into dust bowls or barren hillsides. It is time to halt the stockpiling of our beef, our butter and our weapons of mass destruction. All these will be obsolete if we do survive.

(iii) The Future

> "The growth of compassion for animals during the last few decades will come to be recognised as one of the most amazing and one of the most seminal developments of our times." — Kathleen Jannaway

I do not wish to underestimate the enormous changes needed to bring about a peaceable future; it would certainly take more than just a swing to veganism, though that would be a good and necessary start. Massive changes to the whole socio-economic set-up are needed, and a whole new way of looking at the situation.

£2 billion would finance a worldwide citizens' programme to plant several billion trees each year in a realistic programme of reafforestation — this is approximately the cost of ONE nuclear-armed submarine.[62] Often quoted statements like these summarise the gross misplacement of our resources, but by putting the problem in money terms they perhaps oversimplify, implying that if we stopped spending money on armaments then the world's starving would somehow automatically be fed, and so on. It is in fact the ghastly pseudo-logic of economics which has produced starvation in a world of plenty. Surely we need a new economics of resources, not of money, and we need to bring human and environmental factors into the equation. Our true resources lie not in gold bullion and "futures markets" but in the richness of the land and the skill of the people.

"A vegetarian diet is the acid test of humanitarianism" — Leo Tolstoy

For those of us who are now vegan, the pioneering work has already been done by those who lived as vegans long before we had a wide network of wholefood shops. This was before official research had confirmed the soundness of the diet, so we owe a debt of gratitude to those who started the Vegan Society and produced the *Vegan Journal* in the early decades — the only guidance then available for new vegans. Indeed we are "standing on the shoulders of giants" and it is relatively easy for us to achieve this more humane lifestyle which aims at an equitable distribution of the world's resources.

For the point is not just that animals are suffering in many bizarre and horrific ways. It is not even that it is to our own material benefit that we stop the wasteful and unhealthy business of exploiting animals. But it is for our eventual progression to a more civilised way of living. As long as we have a society which condones people who stand on a production line slaughtering animals, people who perform vivisection, and people who can laugh at the pathetic unnatural antics of circus animals, we will never have a just and peaceful society. What really worries me about these dreadful acts of animal abuse is that there are actually people prepared and willing to carry them out — perhaps the same kind of people who operated the gas chambers.

People who think they are working for peace whilst still eating animal products, or who think they can forget the issue of animal rights and concentrate on human rights, have not got down to the roots of the problem. When people say that they have no time for animal rights in a world which is so lacking in human rights, I wonder just what it is that they are doing 24 hours a day for human rights that prevents them from simply becoming vegetarian — perhaps the most influential single step, to improve the world for humans and animals, that anyone can take — and one that need not take up extra time or money.

Many agree with me and in Britain, Vegetarian Society figures for 1991 show that 7% of the population call themselves vegetarian. Amongst teenagers the proportion of vegetarians is reckoned to be 8%. With the 1984 estimate being only 2%, this represents rapid growth.

This is heartening, because it shows that human growth, as opposed to economic growth, is taking place. If we want to feed the world's hungry, solve balance of payments problems and improve our health, then we must stop the heartless and unnecessary business of exploiting animals. It is the next step forward, though it will come by eventual depletion of resources, whether we like it or not. How much better to come to it not via dire poverty and distress but through heightened sensitivity and health, working for equitable use of Earth's resources, an improvement in our environment and an eventual elimination of warfare.

"Until he extends the circle of his compassion to all living things, man will not himself find peace"
— Albert Schweitzer

When the vegan diet becomes widely adopted and it is generally realised that we no longer need to use animals as food, a whole range of by-products of the slaughterhouse will cease to appear in our other consumer goods, including clothing, footwear, car tyres, photographic film and toiletries. It is well within the range of our ingenuity to produce fabrics and commodities from vegetable and some mineral resources which would be cheap and (unlike some present-day synthetics) ecologically sound.

As we wind down the whole business of animal exploitation, perspectives will shift and we will cease to exploit
animals in any way. The falseness of vivisection as a model
for medicine will be exposed; we would never dream of
using, let along killing, animals for our entertainment or
sport; the vegan landscape could release large tracts of land
to be wild or near-wild, where animals (including people)
could roam free. We might even achieve a paradise in which
animals had lost their fear of us.[63]

All these reforms, bringing with them massive improvements in our environment, would eventually and naturally
follow on from the most basic premise of veganism, which is
to refrain from using animals as food. On a wide and general
level, as well as the individual one, there is a lot of truth in
the thought that we are, or we become, what we eat.

CHAPTER EIGHT

HOW TO EAT VEGAN

The aims of veganism, then, are very high indeed, but we have to start somewhere and in this case it is at the kitchen table and as early as infancy.[64] The meat and milk myth takes root in our tender formative years. Most die-hard meat-eaters are unwilling to give up the stuff that their mothers probably spent hours if not years trying to persuade them to eat; who would sever the sacred bond of motherhood? Meat is an unnatural food for infants and infants have a natural awareness of this. That is why commercial infant "dinners" have an astonishing array of flavourings to tempt the tiny palate. But after the tricky weaning period (tricky for omnivores that is) they have been successfully conditioned, and conditioning is often difficult to eradicate. It would seem almost sacrilegious to deny what one's mother gave one as the very stuff of life.

However, in my own case, once I had become aware of the case for veganism, though it took decades to get there, I changed my diet immediately with no ill effects other than nostalgia. I know many others who have done the same. (Though if you have a "delicate digestion" there is probably something wrong with you already through a lifetime's body abuse, in which case a gradual change-over would probably be better.)

Similarly and perhaps especially with milk, a lifetime's habit can be an enormous obstacle to change. Calling up memories of early childhood comforts, cocoa at bedtime and mother's milk itself, milky drinks provide a subconscious womblike cosiness to those addicted to white tea and coffee. However it is only in comparatively recent times that cow's milk has become big business, and we don't actually need a white fluid on our cereals and in our beverages. But if we can't kick the habit we can easily buy soya "milks" off the shelf.

Soya milk is getting relatively cheaper all the time as more and more people are buying it, but it is still relatively expensive, partly because of the unfair excise duties on the soya ingredient — in terms of Earth's resources each pint should cost only a few pence. It is a great pity that, as well as paying an artificially high price for soya milk, vegans are actually paying through taxation to keep the price of cow's milk artificially low. And low-income vegans, of course, cannot benefit from welfare milk tokens. It is possible to make your own soya "milks" for use in cooking and on cereals by blending porridge oats or ground cashew nuts into water, with a little oil, though they do not mix with acidic tea or coffee.

Tea and coffee, in fact, are cash crops with a long history of injustice, but as they are drugs rather than food they are not really the concern of this book (though soya milk does make a nice cup of tea). Herb teas, wines, fruit cordials and some beers are much healther drinks — not forgetting water, the healthiest and most natural of all. As for the nutritional value of milk, I have already shown that we can get our protein, calcium, vitamins and minerals in abundance from the plant world, avoiding the risks of saturated fat and chemical residues in cow's milk. And, bearing in mind what food is "natural", we should remember that cooking itself is fairly unnatural, and factory-processed foods a complete aberration!

All the nutrients we need for health are provided in abundance by plants. The chart at the end of this book could be greatly extended if space permitted. Using combinations of vegetables, cereals, pulses, fruits and salads, endlessly tasty, colourful and varied meals can be made which get right away from the dull meat-and-two-veg syndrome. In breaking away from the cycle of suffering and exploitation involved in meat production, we throw off old habits of thought in more areas than one, and especially in the kitchen. We need not be creatures of habit, at the mercy of the giants of the food industry.

People who cook need to get away from the idea of recipes as such. Unlike the serfs who threw off their chains only in order to share the indulgences of their rulers, we need to throw off the chains which tell us, through clever marketing, what to wear, what to think, and what to eat. The meat and milk myth has led to the narrow vision of meat and its accompaniments, and a whole way of thinking of a meal as a set piece, following certain conventions, which has to be prepared and served "correctly" according to a recipe which usually somebody else has thought up. The set-piece meals described in popular magazines are a pathetic substitute for creative cooking based on what is in your local shop, your garden and your cupboard.

Having become vegan and thereby taken up responsibility for what we consume, we can now shake off the chains of the "right" and the "wrong" way of going about one of our most vital activities. Having learned what we need to consume in order to be healthy, and having found out how the various foods react when mixed, blended, heated etc. (both endless and fascinating studies in themselves), we can now cook actively, not passively, and with energetic individuality. We can read recipes for ideas and to find out what other people eat, but follow them once only at most, to learn how ingredients behave with each other. The essence of our liberation from the conformity which promotes the myth is to know what we are doing. Awareness is all. Once we know what we are doing, there is usually no need to follow to the last gram or even to measure any ingredient at all, after we have learned what certain amounts look like. It's much quicker to tip food straight from the jar or packet; it saves time and washing up and is thereby another aspect of our liberation.

(ii) Outline of a Vegan Diet

What, then, do we eat, you may say? There are many varieties of vegan diets, from those which include a large proportion of raw food, via wholefood diets through to those which use a lot of convenience foods and packaged foods. They are all unquestionably cheaper than a meat and dairy based diet, even if you buy over-priced soya milk and a few convenience foods.

There is no question of a vegan diet having to be austere or boring; if there is any problem it is that the Western world has been blinded by the over-indulgence in haute cuisine (fat laced with more fat) and, later, cuisine minceur (how to control your fat intake whilst eating as much meat as possible). The high fibre, low fat diet that we now know is good for us is in fact similar to the traditional diets of Southern Europe, India, China, North Africa and South-East Asia — so it includes some of the finest cuisines in the world. Though we cannot leap immediately to such exotic heights (and in any case we may want to avoid using many imported foods), we can adapt our ideas on meals with "foreign" ideas on combinations and flavourings, using food that is available in our shops and gardens.

Try to aim for variety and then you will almost certainly get all the nutrients you need. Foods which taste good together often work well together from a nutritional point of view — for instance, vitamin C and iron (orange juice and muesli, fruit and nuts), vitamin D and oil with calcium (bread and margarine) etc.

Getting into the habit of sprouting seeds is a great nutritional benefit. Punch holes in the top of a dark wide-lidded jar and fill to about one fifth of its depth with mung beans, soya beans, chick peas or alfalfa seeds. Soak them in water for about 24 hours, and afterwards rinse often, using the perforated lid to drain off the water. Keep them in a fairly warm place if possible — the kitchen window-sill will do in summer. After a few days they will be delicious in stir-fried vegetables, or in salads. They are an incredibly good and cheap source of vitamin C, calcium, phosphorous and iron and very easily digestible because the starch in the beans converts to sugar during sprouting.

Nuts are very nutritious and you can make them into lots of different roasts and rissoles — though they are even more nutritious eaten raw. But don't worry if you don't eat nuts very often because you don't like them, or because they are too expensive (and here again, nuts are expensive only because of market forces, not because they are a rare commodity). Cereals, pulses and vegetables are also good sources of protein. There is an extremely wide and colourful selection of dried peas and beans to choose from, to brighten up your kitchen shelves and make endless varieties of bean salads, casseroles, roasts and rissoles. Wash them first, and change the water during cooking if possible if you find they cause flatulence. This is nothing to worry about from a health point of view and is perfectly natural since the healthy human gut, which is designed for a process of fermentation, consists of a proportion of solids and a proportion of gases.

Soya flour is very nutritious and a little can be thrown in with almost anything you are making. A vegan "cheese" can be made by stirring into margarine or vegetable oil as much soya flour as it will take, and flavouring it with Barmine or herbs, etc. — chopped fresh chives are my favourite for this in summer. You can of course buy several different "cheese" spreads in whole food shops, and even soya-based hard cheeses. Tofu is also a useful convenience food, since it has the highest ratio of protein to calories of any known food. You can blend it with margarine, lemon, vanilla and sugar to make a cheesecake, or simply use it as it is in a stir-fry. Packets of commercially sold tofu often give intriguing recipes.

For replacing eggs in a cake, you could use a teaspoon of arrowroot for binding, a dessertspoon of soya flour for food value and baking powder as a raising agent (for a light cake use oil instead of margarine). Or just use one of the many vegan cake recipes now available.

A little on the negative side. Apart from animal fats, sugar is possibly one of the most harmful substances we knowingly consume, for reasons which are now widely known, and so should be largely avoided. Puddings are a tradition which dates back to times when poorer families had to fill up on stodge when their main meal could not provide enough calories, and so should not really be a part of a healthy meal except on special occasions. Salt, too, is a product which enlightened cooks now use very sparingly, as natural foods already have a perfect balance of mineral salts, and an extra intake of sodium chloride upsets the mineral balance of our bodies — overconsumption of salt raises the blood pressure and is now linked with heart disease.

I am aware that I have not adequately answered the question of what vegans do eat. When people confront me with this, imagining that the absence of meat, etc. leaves a large gap, I find it not very easy to answer when put on the spot. I therefore pinned a sheet of paper above my cooker and wrote down each day for two weeks what we were having for the main meal. The result of this may provide others with a few ideas for meals. Listed after that are a few more ideas taken directly from what we eat at our house — other vegans of course will eat quite differently. And near the end of the book there is a section of foolproof recipes, to start off with if necessary.

(iii) Main Meals Over a Typical Fortnight (Summer)

♦ ♦ ♦

BEAN GOULASH WITH NEW POTATOES
AND TOMATO SALAD

For the goulash, fry onions and herbs in paprika (a generous amount) with oil, then add tomato puree, tomatoes, stock, etc. to make a rich sauce in which you then simmer chopped green beans. Heavily flavour the tomato salad with garlic and add a generous amount of parsley. ("Stock" to a vegan is not cube shaped but consists of water extracted from boiled vegetables, or simply a vegetable extract stirred into hot water — Bisto powder, too, is vegan.)

♦ ♦ ♦

MINCE WITH BUBBLE AND SQUEAK

For the mince, fry onions with left-over diced vegetables, add stock and soya mince (TVP) or chopped nuts, and simmer. Meanwhile fry the bubble and squeak (usually mashed potato and cabbage with marge, salt and pepper and a dash of soya milk) until nice and crisp.

GOLDEN FRITTERS WITH
SWEET AND SOUR MARROW

My golden fritters are made from sweet corn, tipped into a small amount of spiced batter and dropped by the spoonful into hot oil. The "sweet and sour" of the sauce (based as usual on fried onions with stock, thickened with flour and tomato puree) is achieved with molasses, soy sauce and cider vinegar (about 1 dsp of each) — simmer the chopped marrow in the sauce.

* * *

'SAUSAGES', CHIPS AND BEANS

Various vegan sausage mixes and sausages are obtainable in health food shops. They also make delicious sausage rolls, pies etc. Because they are relatively expensive I usually increase the bulk of sausage mixes with boiled onions, using the water from the boiling to make the actual mix and sometimes adding left-over cooked rice or breadcrumbs.

* * *

NUT CUTLETS, RICE,
VEGETABLES IN SAUCE, SALAD

There are many types of nut rissoles, etc., but basically the mix consists of ground nuts, herbs, porridge oats (or breadcrumbs or wholemeal flour) for increasing the bulk, soya flour for richness, chopped onions, often fried first, for a savoury flavour and Barmine for B12 (add a huge teaspoon for flavour at the end of cooking to any savoury sauce). The rissole mixture holds together by the porridge oats absorbing the water and binding the other ingredients. Mould and squeeze it firmly with your hands (it can also be baked).

BEAN ROAST, CHILLI SAUCE, SALAD, POTATOES

I usually do roast potatoes in the top of the oven when making any kind of roast. A quick roast can be made with tinned butter beans mashed up with tomatoes, herbs (e.g. rosemary, basil), oil, chopped onions and a little wholemeal flour or porridge oats. Barmine of course. This mixture is shaped into a dome and placed in the centre of the oven, smoothed over with oil or marge and often surrounded by whole parboiled onions and root vegetables. For the sauce, three finely chopped dried chillies added to a sauce based on onions, garlic and tomatoes will be hot enough for most people. Serve all this with a salad which is mainly green. This is a popular meal which I often give to guests.

* * *

PIZZA AND SALAD

I usually make a huge savoury scone with white self-raising flour (adding wheat germ and soya flour to salve my conscience), a little oil, salt and water, and fry it very gently in a cast-iron pan. The topping usually consists of chopped vegetables in a sauce flavoured with oregano, and this is spread over the huge scone pizza while the second side is cooking (it should be at least 5cm thick to serve three or four). Olives are delicious with this.

* * *

STEW AND DUMPLINGS

Always start a stew off by frying the onions and garlic. This prevents sticking on the bottom of the pan later. Dark green leaves are often an ingredient of my stews, and one or more of the dried pulses. Chick peas, spinach and tomato are a good combination. Dumplings are very popular (there is also a sweet version of dumplings, cooked in fruit whilst it is stewing).

PEASE PUDDING, POTATOES,
SALAD — THEN A DESSERT

We like pease pudding hot or cold (hummus is the Eastern version) and it's useful at lunchtime. I often serve it warmed up with roasted vegetables and a hot chilli sauce. This meal was deliberately light because I had made a REFRIGER-ATED CHOCOLATE CAKE for a treat to follow — crushed vegan biscuits stirred into a mixture of melted dark chocolate, margarine, cocoa and whipped vegan cream, cooled in the fridge and topped with more vegan cream and almonds.

◄ ◄ ◄

MOUSSAKA

One version of this dish consists of new potatoes and aubergines, casseroled in a rich herby sauce of tomatoes, onions and garlic. Towards the end of cooking a white sauce is poured over and it is served when this is golden and bubbling.

◄ ◄ ◄

RICE BALLS, SPICY SAUCE, SALAD

Cooked rice squeezed into balls (add a bit of flour if it won't hold together), coated with sesame seeds and fried, is very tasty.

◄ ◄ ◄

PASTY, ROAST POTATOES, SALAD AND SAUCE

I often make a pie, or if I have time individual pasties, from left-over vegetables mixed with TVP, onions, Barmine and enough water to moisten. Naturally you would cook something else — potatoes for instance — in the oven at the same time. (I also make a variation of flapjack nearly every time the oven is on, as this gets eaten up rapidly — it usually contains sesame seeds and currants for their nutritional value.)

RATATOUILLE

Many books will have versions of this, and it should be vegan anyway. It goes well with very fresh bread and new or roast potatoes, depending on the season.

❧ ❧ ❧

CURRY

You could easily fill a book with vegan curries alone. I often make a hot dahl, or lentil curry, which cooks during the time it takes to boil brown rice, so the whole thing can be ready in not much more than half an hour. The fresh salad part of a meal is always welcome with a hot curry, even if it's only chopped onions and/or tomatoes. I usually serve at least chopped onions dressed with mint sauce with most curries.

(iv) Some More Ideas for Meals
(also see recipes)

❧ ❧ ❧

SHEPHERD'S PIE

Cooked vegetables in a sauce — for instance the 'mince' already described topped with mashed potatoes and casseroled.

❧ ❧ ❧

CASSEROLED vegetables are somehow always more delicious than a stew done on top of the cooker.

❧ ❧ ❧

CHILLI without carne, but with the beans and possibly TVP, is delicious when cooked slowly in the oven, served with fresh bread and a crisp salad.

BOLOGNAISE to pour over your pasta can be made with vegetables cooked in a rich tomato sauce. TVP mince can be added for a nostalgic appearance, but garlic and oregano alone will give it an authentic Bolognaise taste.

♣ ♣ ♣

STUFFED VEGETABLES

Potatoes, peppers, marrows and huge mushrooms are the candidates that spring to mind first. Rice, nuts, breadcrumbs are useful for stuffing, or of course one of the "sausage" mixes. For a treat, a tasty sauce can be poured over the stuffed vegetables and they can be casseroled in this rather than merely baked. A really nice stuffed vegetable is partly boiled cabbage leaves which are rolled around the stuffing and then baked with tomato sauce poured all round them in the dish.

♣ ♣ ♣

PANCAKES

Sweet or savoury, stuffed and rolled or piled up with filling spread between.

♣ ♣ ♣

PÂTÉS

Lentil pate, hummus, pease pudding can be used in various ways e.g. eaten straight with vegetables or salad, as sandwich filling, in pasties or pâté en croute etc.

♣ ♣ ♣

CHINESE VEGETABLES

A variety of vegetables chopped into slivers and cooked quickly in a little oil before serving. (Personally I don't often do this action cooking because I like to relax with a glass of wine before eating.)

SALADS

Don't forget fruits, nuts and pulses as salad ingredients, and also cooked vegetables you wouldn't normally associate with a salad (for instance, lightly cooked broccoli with sliced avocado in a vinaigrette dressing makes a delicious green salad). Also, try to include the various parts of plants, such as roots, shoots, leaves and fruit. Be adventurous! Try things like celery and walnuts, cooked rice and orange slices, apples, celery and beans, and of course in summer, young dandelion leaves. If green is not part of the salad itself, then serve the salad on a bed of leaves.

❦ ❦ ❦

WILD FOODS

Even without specialist knowledge, many people are in a position to take advantage of dandelion greens and nettles (each spring we have a soup made from the fresh young tops of the first crop of nettles). These are plentiful and very nutritious especially compared with anaemic shop-bought lettuce. Never pick from the roadside since plants absorb lead from passing vehicles through the leaves. If you have time you can read up on wild food and do a bit of exploring in your own area. The classic wild ingredients such as dandelion, nettle and elderberry are plentiful even in the city.

CHAPTER NINE

VEGAN BABIES

Another bonus of being vegan is that it reduces some of our qualms about having children (only some of the qualms!). Since vegans use far less of the Earth's resources than do omnivores, population pressures are seen in a different light (though Westerners, whether vegan or not, still consume far more resources than people in the poor world). Children raised on a sensible vegan diet are attractive and full of vitality.

(i) The Easy Approach

As vegans, we believe that our diet which excludes animal products is most akin to what "natural" food for humans might be. It certainly need not lack any essential nutrients and we are not doing without vital or useful foods. Therefore weaning vegan babies is perfectly easy and natural. Indeed I have noticed that many of the infant feeding problems which fill the pages of popular magazines are often associated with well-meaning mothers forcing meat and cow's milk down unwilling little throats.

In our society at this particular time, milk especially has wheedled its way into all kinds of foods and drinks and is particularly associated with infants and children. But for vegans, cow's milk as it appears in bottles for human consumption is an abhorrent substance, and we feel that it cannot possibly be a natural drink for us. I have no qualms whatever about letting my children go without it; indeed to make them drink it would seem to me an aberration. Certainly a child who has not been weaned onto milk finds the taste repugnant.

It is true that when school milk was introduced in Britain, the mass consumption of milk by young children relieved the symptoms of severe undernourishment, like rickets, which were widespread at the time amongst underprivileged children. But it was wrong to assume that milk was the magic ingredient to combat malnourishment; it was simply the food that was used at the time, for reasons of convenience to politicians and farmers (often the same people). And now that milk is being discredited as a healthy drink even in orthodox medical circles, it is a pity that it still retains somewhere in folk memory an image of being "good for us".

The thing about vegan infant feeding is not that it is specialist or difficult in any way, but only that it differs from the norm, at present, in our society. The difficulty lies not with the vegan diet but outside it, when most books on babies, and infant foods available, assume an omnivorous diet. Vegan foods are a minority amongst the masses of proprietary infant foods now available. Special baby foods in jars and cans, of course, are another marketing confidence trick and are not necessary at all. We can easily do without them, and an outline of how to go about this is the purpose of this section of the book.

Weaning vegan babies is perfectly easy and natural and should not present any problem. The real problems come later at butchers' shop windows and perhaps the school dinner table, when the growing child realises that s/he is living in a cruel world.

Every vegan who has gone through pregnancy and lactation will have educated herself as much as possible on vegan nutrition. (Health prior to conception, for both parents, is vital too of course.) A working knowledge of nutrition is the first requirement for weaning your baby, as with omnivores. The second is a little ingenuity in gradually introducing the baby to your normal family foods with the minimum of extra food preparation time.

There are no hard rules on infant weaning since, like many other mammals, human beings are extremely adaptable. Baby feeding patterns and fashions have changed several times in this country even over a period of a decade or two. Nor can we look for guidance as to what might be "natural" to child-rearing customs in other parts of the world, since there are many different patterns, depending on the diet and customs of the locality — the main overall difference being that breast feeding generally continues for a longer period in non-industrialised nations.

Orthodox thinking in this country now seems to be that breast feeding is not only desirable but essential[65] (of course — though incredibly, not so long ago it was presented as merely an option to new mothers) and that by the age of about six months supplementary feeding should be under way, to provide, firstly, additional iron. Interestingly, it is also advised that ordinary cow's milk should not be introduced in the first year — another U-turn by the professionals! Since there are many varieties of vegan diet, there is no one way of weaning vegan babies. It all depends on what the family eats, as the idea is to introduce the new member of the family to a diet similar to everyone else's. You should spend as much time as possible enjoying your baby, and as little as possible preparing food and reading about it.

(ii) Feeding Babies

There are several excellent and easily available books about breast feeding, which may interest you before and during lactation, and there is usually help to hand for any difficulties. The vegan diet is wonderful for sustaining a lactating woman but do make sure you have an intake of vitamin B12, since lack of this vitamin could severely hamper the baby's development. This is the one time that a regular B12 tablet supplement is recommended. As for other nutrients, they will almost certainly be adequately provided in the breast milk, and if your diet is inadequate this is more likely to be at the expense of your own vitaliy, rather that the quality of your milk.

You will find that you are drinking more than normal, so this could be a good time to experiment with different herb teas (raspberry leaf being the classic herb for this period of your life) since drugs like caffeine and alcohol transfer to the milk. Breast feeding is all that is needed for the first few months, and the baby is the best judge of the amount needed and the frequency of feeds. It is impossible to over-feed a breast-fed baby.

Incidentally, proprietary infant feeding formulas are available which are soya based and vegan, though check the labels for animal-derived stereates and vitamin D3 which is derived from lanolin or fish oil (vitamin D2 is vegan though). Ordinary soya milks are fine when babies are weaning and ready to drink from a cup, though obviously it is not sufficient as a sole infant food.

It seems a momentous occasion when one first gives a baby something other than one's own milk. Initially the additional feeding is not intended to provide the baby with basic nutrients, but to get him or her used to the idea of feeding from a spoon, etc., to prepare for when it is needed later. Good foods to use initially are fruits (naturally) and perhaps root vegetables. Sieved ripe bananas, peaches, lightly stewed and sieved apples, prunes, pears and apricots are all suitable. Babies often like root vegetables, especially carrots, and it is likely that root vegetables have been treated with far fewer artificial chemicals than the fruits in the shops. A couple of spoonsful of the cooked strained vegetable are all that is needed at first.

If you want to see if the baby will enjoy drinking from a bottle, you could try offering strained fruit and vegetable juices, like apple and carrot, diluted with warm boiled water, or some fresh orange juice or the juice of soaked raisins. This is not actually necessary if you don't feel inclined to use a bottle, as breast milk provides all the necessary vitamins and fluid — it is a wonderful supply and demand mechanism that you don't have to worry about at all.

Baby cereals are often also recommended as first food — particularly in sales literature. Non-glutenous kinds such as baby rice or Farex baby weaning food would be good ones to try. They can be mixed with a little soya milk and warm boiled water, or some of your own milk if you are good at expressing it. In early times, cereals were pre-masticated by the mother, an excellent way of preparing them for a baby since digestion of starches begins in the mouth with the action of saliva.

By the age of about six months the baby will probably be anticipating and enjoying the solid food, and as s/he approaches the three meals a day routine might possibly be sleeping through the night.

TYPICAL BABY DINNER AT 5-6 MONTHS

1 small potato
half a carrot
piece of cabbage leaf or sprig of parsley

Cover with water and simmer gently until soft. Push through a sieve (including the water) and stir in a tiny dash of yeast extract.

By the age of about six months you may be offering cereal and/or fruit at breakfast time (though not much is needed because you will probably breast feed the baby as soon as you both wake) and later in the day you will be introducing two other meal times. The above suggestion for a baby dinner can be made at lunch-time and half reserved in a clean cup for later, to be reheated in a pan of water (never of course save a part-eaten portion). Small amounts of pulses can now be introduced.

♦ ♦ ♦

TYPICAL MAIN MEAL AT 6-7 MONTHS

1 small potato
half a carrot
small piece of greens
1 dsp other vegetables — parsnips, peas or etc.
1 dsp red lentils (washed)

Cover with water and boil gently until soft. Then add a dash of yeast extract and blend or finely mince the food. This is done instead of sieving as in the early stages, because it retains the fibre, which the baby's system is now ready for, in this pulverised state.

Instead of the pulses, ground nuts could be mixed in, but babies often seem to prefer peas and lentils to nuts. Baby cereal can be mixed in with this vegetable puree, and also some tomato puree, which babies enjoy, and/or a dash of yeast extract.

By seven or eight months, when you are getting fed up with preparing special food for the baby, you will probably find that s/he is now ready to participate in nomal family meals. A good start is:

● ● ●

SOUP OF THE DAY

Fry a small onion in a generous amount of oil. Then add 2–3 cups of chopped vegetables (potatoes, carrots, peas, tomatoes, celery, etc. — enough for the amount you want), half a cup of lentils or other washed pulses (which should have been pre-soaked) and a generous amount of fresh herbs or a pinch of dried herbs. Cover with plenty of water and simmer until soft.

When the vegetables are soft, take out two big scoopfuls for the baby, before adding salt and pepper for the rest of the family. Blenderise the baby's portion for a few seconds only, or mash with a fork. S/he will now be learning to chew, with or without many teeth.

At this stage, pieces of bread can be added to the baby's food instead of baby cereals — the baby may prefer the taste and texture. For the times when the baby is sitting round the table with you, probably in the high chair, you can offer rusks. Several vegan rusks are available, but you can always just use dry toast if you don't want to buy them. By seven or eight months, bread and margarine with a touch of yeast extract will be enjoyed. Young children need plenty of calories and should be allowed to fill themselves up at each meal (but do not of course use food as a substitute for attention between meals)

During this period, the "soup of the day" which you make with the baby in mind can be used in various ways for the main meal if you don't use it at lunch time. It can be transformed into a curry, goulash or bolognaise, or mixed into soya or nutburgers etc. — I have found it a helpful way of minimising preparation time for the evening meal whilst at the same time providing two main courses for the baby.

Very soon after this stage, by about nine to ten months, the baby will be sharing some of your own meals. Just about all vegan food is palatable to babies — perhaps softened with a little hot water or soya milk — but concentrate on the vegetables only, if you are having a fried or heavily spiced dish.

Weaning is usually a gradual process and should be done not by the parent but by the baby. In my opinion babies should be allowed to breast feed for as long as they wish. After all, babies are the only humans who retain a completely natural intuition about what is good for them. If you allow the baby to wean him/herself then you will almost certainly continue to breast feed well into the second year, often much longer. (But by this time of course the baby's solid food provides the bulk of nourishment and feeding is not so frequent as with small babies.)

There should not be any problems in child feeding associated specifially with veganism. Remember that in proportion to body weight, children's protein requirements are far greater than adults'. Soya drinks and foods are invaluable for this reason and most children will like them when nicely presented — possibly in naturally flavoured drinks, fruit mousses and soyaburgers, all of which are classics for children.

(iii) Children's Parties

Children's parties are about giving our children a real day to remember and unless it's a disaster, food will not be the main memory. However it's a good opportunity to show off attractive vegan fare. And in fact the best way to throw a party for strangers is to provide vegan food — there is no way you can offend those who need kosher, halal or vegetarian food; vegan truly is the universal base line.

Children need something they can easily recognise and relate to, so this is not a good time to try your sugar-free, wholemeal recipes. A basic sponge cake can be baked in special shaped tins or cut up to make fancy shapes. No children's party is complete without sausages on sticks, and all children seem to like proprietary vegan sausages and sosmix made into sausage rolls, etc. You can even get vegan jellies (the kosher one is the best) and ice cream these days. Try to have lots of small items for children to pick at — savoury snacks and nibbles, sticks of cucumber, celery, carrot and tomato. Put out lots of seasonal fruit and you may be surprised how well it goes down. Older children will appreciate a nonalcoholic punch made with fruit juices, sparkling mineral water, fruit pieces and ice cubes.

Eating, after all, should be enjoyable, and children should grow up with memories of many happy mealtimes. If we could effect a large-scale changeover to a vegan diet, then perhaps we could all eat our fill without our happiness being clouded by the knowledge that in global terms we are a privileged minority.

RECISES

(with thanks to Dawn Dakin for her
chocolate cake and flapjack)

* * *

HIGH PROTEIN ROAST

1 large onion	*1 dsp yeast extract*
60–80g mushrooms	*1 tbs soy sauce*
110g red lentils	*1 tbs lemon juice*
110g ground nuts	*2 tbs oil*
80g breadcrumbs	*seasoning to taste*
1 tbs wheatgerm	*1 tsp dried herbs*

Wash the lentils and cook in water until soft. Meanwhile chop the onions and mushrooms and fry in oil. When soft, add all the rest of the ingredients and mix well. Shape into a mound on a greased baking tray, brush with oil and bake at 200ºC for 30 mins.

A mild olive oil is nutritionally best for cooking because it changes its chemical composition at a higher temperature than most other common cooking oils.

A layer of sliced tomatoes can be sandwiched in the middle of this roast before baking, for variety. I usually surround a roast with partially cooked root vegetables and baste the whole in oil during cooking. Nut roast of course can be eaten cold afterwards, though left-overs are unlikely.

STEAMED SAVOURY
KATE AND SIDNEY PUDDING

Filling:
1 small cup dried
   butter beans
1 tbs oil
2 tomatoes or
   some tomato puree
1 onion, chopped
4 or 5 mushrooms
half tsp mixed dried herbs
1 tbs soy sauce
pepper to taste

Crust:
6 heaped tbs SR flour
1 heaped tbs wheat germ
1 heaped tbs soya flour
pinch salt
3 tbs vegetable oil
cold water

Soak the beans overnight and simmer until soft — 40–45 mins. (Or open a tin of cooked butter beans.)

Filling — fry the onion in oil with the herbs. Add mushrooms and tomato puree. When heated through, add beans, soya sauce and seasoning and simmer gently whilst preparing the crust.

Crust — combine all ingredients together in a bowl, mixing and kneading with fingers of one hand. Add enough cold water to make a firm pastry consistency. Lightly grease a 20cm pudding basin and press two thirds of the pastry round the inside. Tip in the filling and form a sealed top with the rest of the pastry. Cut a small hole in the middle of the pastry lid. Place in a large saucepan in 5 cm boiling water and cover with an inverted dish or smaller saucepan lid, to prevent the top getting soaked. Cover the large saucepan with its own lid and steam for 35-40 mins. (don't let the water dry up).

Serve with potatoes, gravy and a green vegetable.

BEANBURGERS

1 tin red kidney beans or
   1 mug cooked beans,
   well rinsed
1 onion, finely shopped
1 tbs dried parsley or a
   generous handful fresh
   chopped parsley

1 tbs wholemeal flour
1 dsp lemon juice
1 dsp soy sauce
2 tbs tomato puree
salt and pepper

Mash the beans thoroughly, then mix in all the other
ingredients, blending with a little water if necessary to
achieve a stiff paste consistency. Form into flat round
shapes and fry gently in a generous amount of oil until a rich
brown colour.

Serve with chips, tomatoes and white bread rolls.
Follow with a fruit sorbet.

🍎 🍎 🍎

HOME MADE SAUSAGE MIX

100g breadcrumbs
100g finely chopped nuts
100g flavoured TVP mince
2 tbs mixed herbs
1 tbs soya flour

2 tbs tomato puree in 1 cup
   hot water
1 dsp yeast extract
1 tbs wheat germ

Mix all ingredients together. Stand for a few minutes before
frying. Keeps for a couple of days in the fridge.
This is also nice for stuffing huge tomatoes — put a dot of
marge on top and bake at 190ºC for 20 mins.

Shop bought sosmix can be varied by
— adding tomato paste to the mixture
— adding finely chopped garlic and herbs
— coating in sesame seeds before frying
— boiling a chopped onion in water and using
to make the mix.

RISOTTO

Boil 1 cup brown rice in 2 cups water very gently for 35–40 mins until all the water is absorbed — or follow instructions on the packet. Meanwhile cook gently in another pan:

1 chopped onion
2 tbs oil
1 sliced green or red pepper
1 tsp curry powder
ADD
cooked rice
1 can sweetcorn
half cup salted peanuts

Stir together. Serve with tomatoes, fresh salad and crusty bread.

● ● ●

CRISPY LAYERED MUSHROOMS

225g wholemeal breadcrumbs   *225g mushrooms*
125g milled nuts   *225g tomatoes*
125g marge   *salt and pepper*
1 large onion   *1 tsp dried marjoram*
                                                          or mixed herbs

Combine nuts and breadcrumbs. Melt most of the marge and fry bread & nut mixture until golden. Chop onion and sautee in the rest of the marge until transparent. Add remaining ingredients and simmer gently for 5 mins. Lightly grease an ovenproof dish and layer up the breadcrumbs and vegetables, starting and finishing with a layer of bread mixture.
Bake at 190ºC for half an hour.
Serve with vegetables and gravy in winter, salad in summer.

HOT CHILLI SAUCE

1 tbs oil	*half tsp dried mixed herbs*
2-3 dried chilli peppers	*or basil*
1 onion	*1 dsp wholemeal flour*
1 clove garlic	*half cup water*
1 large (400g) can tomatoes	*soy sauce*

Chop onion and garlic finely and fry in oil, in a saucepan. Add herbs and chopped chillis. Dissolve flour in a cup of water, add to pan and stir. Add canned tomatoes, with juice, crushing them with spoon. Simmer until the meal is ready (at least 10 mins). Add soy sauce to taste (instead of salt).

A quick "sweet and sour" sauce can be made as above, omitting the chillis and adding 1 tbs molasses or black treacle, and 1 tbs vinegar or lemon juice.

● ● ●

MUSHROOM AND ALMOND QUICHE

Line a flan ring with wholemeal pastry (or vegan frozen pastry which is easily available in supermarkets)

Chop and fry a large onion in 30ml vegetable oil, then add 225g chopped mushrooms and continue frying for five more minutes. Remove from the heat and mix in:

2 tbs soya flour	*1 tsp yeast extract*
100g ground almonds	*1 tsp dried mixed herbs*
225g breadcrumbs	*pinch salt and pepper*

Press down in the pastry case and level the top, sprinkling with a few lefover breadcrumbs. Decorate the top with a few whole almonds and bake for 35 mins at 190ºC.

LENTIL PÂTÉ

220g lentils
60g breadcrumbs or
  porridge oats
1 finely chopped onion

2 tbs oil
large pinch dried sage
0.3l water or stock
seasoning

Fry onions with sage in oil in a saucepan. Add lentils and water or stock, When lentils are mushy and liquid absorbed, take off heat, add breadcrumbs or oats (enough to make the right consistency) and seasoning. Mix well and leave to cool in a nice dish.

This is good in sandwiches and is also useful in pasties etc. You can even form it into rissoles, coat with flour and fry it.

❦ ❦ ❦

PEASE PUDDING

1 cup dried split green peas
1 onion
1–2 tbs oil

half tsp dried sage or
  dried mixed herbs
salt and pepper

Soak peas overnight of for 1 hour in boiling water. Rinse, then place in a pan with enough water to cover. Simmer 35 mins until soft. Meanwhile finely chop the onion and fry in oil with herbs until soft. Add the mushy peas and stir together thoroughly with seasoning.

❦ ❦ ❦

LEMONY BEAN DIP

Blend together:

1 large tin butter beans
1 tbs water
juice and grated rind
  of 1 small lemon

50g vegan margarine
1 clove garlic, crushed
salt and pepper

without the water this becomes a pâté.

SOYA SPREAD

Great for sandwiches and far cheaper than the stuff that comes in tubes!

Stir into some vegetable oil enough soya flour to produce a spreading consistency. Then add, to taste:

yeast extract, tomato puree, chopped chives or another flavouring of your choice, e.g. chopped fresh mixed herbs, onion powder, ketchup, lime pickle, etc . . .

               🍎 🍎 🍎

DAWN'S INCREDIBLE CHOCOLATE CAKE

225g plain wholemeal flour
25g cocoa powder
125g soft vegan margarine
140ml soya milk and 140ml water, mixed
50g raw cane sugar
1tbs golden syrup
1 tsp bicarbonate of soda
2 tsp baking powder

Set over to 180ºC.

Mix together flour and cocoa, rub in marge as though making pastry until the mixture resembles the texture of breadcrumbs. Stir in sugar, baking powder and bicarb. Add liquid and syrup and stir thoroughly but do not beat. Pour mixture into 2 greased and lined sandwich tins and bake for 30 mins until risen and firm to touch.

Leave to cool for 10 mins in the tins, then carefully remove and cool on a wire rack.

Sandwich together with a mixture of:
60g marge
1 large tbs syrup
a large dsp cocoa

PANCAKES

6 heaped tbs white SR flour	*pinch salt*
1 heaped tbs wheat germ	*water*
1 heaped tbs soya flour	*oil for frying*
1 dsp oil	

Make the batter an hour or two before needed if possible. Put all dry ingredients into a bowl and mix thoroughly. Then stir in the oil and gradually add enough water to form a paste. Beat this paste thoroughly, then gradually stir in more water until a pouring consistency is reached.

Make the pancakes in a hevy pan, using the minimum amount of oil. Pour in the batter when the oil is HOT. Flip the pancakes over with a slice if afraid to toss (or even cook three small pancakes in the pan at the same time — much easier to flip over).

Serve with sugar, syrup, oranges, lemons.
Or fill with Chinese style vegetables and sprouted pulses, for a savoury pancake roll.

♦ ♦ ♦

FRESH FRUIT "SORBET"

Whizz together in a blender chopped fresh fruits in season — with just enough juice to operate the blender. Reserve some whole pieces for decoration (but not apple or banana as they will discolour unless wetted with lemon juice etc.) Chill.

A nice dessert if the meal did not include a large salad.

FRUIT CAKE

Simmer in a saucepan for a few minutes:
1 mug dried fruit
quarter mug sugar
half mug water

Then add:
1 mug SR flour
1 tbs oil
half tsp bicarb of soda
1 tbs soya flour
1 tbs wheat germ

Mix thoroughly. Bake slowly for about 45 mins, until a knife sunk into the cake comes out clean.

The above is based on a war-time recipe devised when eggs were scarce. A much more wholesome rich fruit cake can be made by thoroughly mixing together:
220g plain wholemeal flour
280g dried fruit
3 tbs oil
160g water
Bake slowly for about an hour and a half.

BISCUITS

150g wholemeal flour
half tsp bicarb of soda   1 large tbs syrup
1 tsp ground ginger   50g marge

Melt syrup and marge in a saucepan. Add dry ingredients.
Mix well. Roll into balls and place well apart on a baking
tray. Flatten down with the flat side of the tines of a fork.
Cook until golden at 180ºC. Allow to cool before removing
from tray.

It is very easy to make delicious and light scones and buns,
etc., without eggs or cow's milk. I always add a little soya
flour for nourishment.

Flapjack is another standby which is easily made vegan
(adapt any recipe). Nuts, seeds, etc., can be added for extra
nourishment.

♦ ♦ ♦

DAWN'S POPPY SEED FLAPJACKS

75g raw cane sugar   225g rolled oats
2 tbs golden syrup   1tbs poppy seeds
125g marge

Set oven to 180ºC.
Melt the marge with the sugar & syrup. Then stir in the
rolled oats and the poppy seeds and mix thoroughly. Turn
into a greased shallow square tin, and smooth the top with
a knife. Bake for 25–30 mins until golden brown.
    Cool in the tin for 2 mins, then cut into fingers. Cool
completely before removing from the tin.

QUICK CHUTNEY

275g stoneless dates
275g sultanas
275g cooking apples,
  peeled and cored
275g onions
275g raw sugar

0.3 litre vinegar
half tsp salt
3 tbs black molasses
half tsp pepper
1 tsp ground ginger

Finely chop or mince together all the solid ingredients, then stir in the liquids and spices.

Allow to stand, lightly covered, in a large bowl for 24 hours then bottle as usual (makes 3–4 large jars).

I always make chutney this way because it saves fuel and does not fill the kitchen with steam. It keeps just as well — at least a year.

Another delicious chutney is made on the above principle using the spent elderberries left after wine-making — they are still very rich in minerals.

Chutney is a very good accompaniment to nut roasts.

NUTRIENTS CHART

PROTEIN	Nuts (pistachios, almonds & brazils especially), soya beans & products especially tofu, cereals, whole grains, wheat germ, dried peas and beans, brewer's yeast, sunflower seeds, sesame seeds, pumpkin seeds, avocados, peanuts, potatoes, spinach, dried apricots
CARBO-HYDRATES	Bread, cereals, pulses, nuts, potatoes
FATS	Vegetable oils especially olive oil, soya, rapeseed, walnut and linseed oils, nuts, margarines, some vegetables, eg avocado
CALCIUM	Molasses, almonds, brazils, baked beans, tofu, wholemeal bread, sunflower seeds, dried fruits, beetroot, dark green leaves especially spinach, parsley, watercress, sesame seeds, dried peas and beans, turnips, carob flour, dried figs, fortified soya milk, some spices (the seeds), soya flour, oatmeal, pumpkin seeds, edible seaweeds
IRON	Molasses, oatmeal, lentils, millet, tofu, dark green leaves especially spinach, parsley, dried fruits, sunflower seeds, sesame seeds, soya flour, wholemeal bread, figs, apricots, brewer's yeast, bran, wheat germ, baked beans, soya beans, almonds, brazils, cashews, pistachios, cocoa, apricots, hazel nuts, peas, whole cereals, pumpkin seeds, dried fruits, edible seaweed
FOLIC ACID	Raw green leafy vegetables, yeast & yeast extracts, nuts and whole grains

VITAMIN A	Carrots, dark greens, tomatoes, pears, lettuce, brussels sprouts, peas, margarine, peppers, spinach, watercress, cabbage, dried apricots, prunes, turnip tops, kale, parsley, sweet potatoes, mangos
B VITAMINS	All the whole cereals and grains, pulses, yeast extracts, oatmeal, potatoes, beer, wheat germ
VITAMIN B12	Yeast extracts, many processed foods, eg Sosmix, breakfast cereals — check the label, tempeh, miso
VITAMIN C	Raw fruit and vegetables, especially rosehips, blackcurrants, cabbage and all greens, oranges, all citrus fruits, green peppers, mango, tomatoes, kiwi fruits
VITAMIN D	Sunlight, margarine, some fortified foods (check the label)
VITAMIN E	Whole cereals, pulses, vegetable oils, wheat germ, green vegetables, tofu, nuts
VITAMIN K	Green vegetables, pulses and grains

REFERENCES

1. Jeremy Rifkin, *Beyond Beef: The Rise and Fall of the Cattle Culture*. (Published in the US by E P Dutton 1992 and quoted in *The Geographical Magazine* July 1992.)

2. Jon Bennett and Susan George, *The Hunger Machine* (Polity Press 1987).

3. "Over £25 million will be spent on advertising and promoting meat this year" — *Meat Trades Journal* 25 April 1991.

4. F. Wokes, *Plant Foods for Human Nutrition* 1.32, 1968.

5. W J Bray in *New Scientist*, April 1976.

6. J T Coppock, *Agricultural Geography*.

7. BBC News announcement 29 January 1992.

8. Figures from Oxfam.

9. J Rifkin, op cit.

10. Geoffrey Cannon, *The Politics of Food* (Century 1988).

11. Caroline Walker and Geoffrey Cannon, *The Food Scandal* (Century 1984).

12. *Vegan Journal*, vol 31, no 2.

13. *The Western Morning News*, 16 September 1982.

14. South-Western Water Authority Report, September 1982.

15. National Rivers Authority Fact File, 1991.

16. Info and demonstration from the Centre for Alternative Technology, Machynlleth, Powys SY20 9AZ.

17. Details from the Henry Doubleday Research Association, National Centre for Organic Gardening, Ryton-on-Dunsmore, Coventry CV8 3LG.

18. Letter from the Faculty of Technology, Open University, to K. Jannaway November 1986. Similarly, a letter from the Henry Doubleday Research Association states, "I do not know of any nutrients that are generally not found in plant compost which are in manures".

19. FAO figures from 1974.

20. Ministry of Agriculture leaflet.

21. J H Kellog quoted in *Food For a Future* — see Bibliography.

22. At Ploughshares in Glastonbury — 54 Roman Way, Glastonbury, BA6 8AD.

23. The Medway report, sponsored by the RSPCA, was researched by a group of distinguished scientists and published in 1979. Available through the RSPCA.

24. Compassion in World Farming report — The Welfare of Farmed Fish, 1992.

25. P Wells & M Jetter, *The Global Consumer* (Gollancz 1991).

26. J Bronowski, *The Ascent of Man* (BBC Publications 1973).

27. There is an interesting section on the health of various people who traditionally have a high intake of animal produce, like the Innuit and the Masai, in *Food for a Future* — see Bibliography.

28. *Diet, Lifestyle and Mortality in China* reviewed in *New Scientist*, January 1991. The survey also shows that vegetarians show no sign of anaemia, that vegans have average rates of osteoporosis and that a high fibre diet does not inhibit iron intake.

29. In my home town, two children have just spent five weeks in hospital after drinking unpasteurised milk, and are now waiting to find out if they need kidney transplants.

30. Gill Langley, *Vegan Nutrition*, Vegan Society 1988.

31. *New Scientist*, August 1992.

32. Gill Langley, op cit.

33. Jon Wynne-Tyson, op cit.

34. Gill Langley, op cit.

35. Alan Lewis, *The Natural Athlete* (Century Publishing 1984).

36. Gill Langley, op cit.

37. Gill Langley, op cit.

38. Jonathan S Christie, *Food for Vitality* (Bantam Books 1992).

39. COMA (Committee on Medical Aspects of Food Policy) Report *Dietary Reference Values for Food Energy and Nutrients for the United Kingdom* (HMSO 1991).

40. Drew Smith, *Guardian*, 17 June 1983.

41. Ronald Blythe, *Guardian*, 4 March 1982.

42. A chicken farmer, quoted in the *Guardian*, 4 March 1992.

43. This information from The Vegetarian Society.

44. *The Veterinary Record* vol III no2, 1982.

45. Dr J Pentreath of the National Rivers Authority — *Guardian*, 17 October 1991.

46. *Daily Telegraph*, 10 August 1991.

47. *Independent on Sunday*, 5 September 1993.

48. The EU has now declared a moratorium on the use of this drug in the dairy industry, but there is no guarantee that the manufacturers Monsanto, the American drug multinational, will not eventually win the day, or that it is not being used in other parts of the world.

49. BBC Horizon, May 1992 — Fast Life in the Food Chain.

50. *Farmers Weekly*, 10 February 1984.

51. BBC Horizon, May 1992.

52. cf. *The Secret Life of Plants* by Peter Tompkins and Christopher Bird (Penguin 1975).

53. Figures from Animal Aid.

54. Figures released by the RSPCA in May 1989 state that 4,000 dogs and cats are destroyed each day.

55. *Katz Go Vegan* — available from the Vegan Society. See contacts list.

56. The most comprehensive and up-to-date book on circuses is *The Rose Tinted Menagerie* by William Johnson (Heretic Books 1990).

57. Jon Wynne-Tyson, *Food For a Future*; John Bryant, *Fettered Kingdoms*.

58. Over 25 per cent of people questioned in a survey conducted by Animal Aid in September 1984 were not aware when eating meat that they were eating a dead animal.

59. H Bailey Stevens quoted in the *Vegan Journal* vol 25 no 4.
60. J Rifkin, op cit.
61. For instance, Sally Eastall, top marathon runner, Carl Lewis, the champion sprinter, and Katharine Monbiot, British women's heavyweight champion armwrestler.
62. *World Military and Social Expenditure* 1991.
63. "Our future survival depends on our ability to recover community with animals" — Kit Pedler, *The Quest for Gaia.*
64. "People have never had freedom of choice in nutrition. With the best of intentions their parents misled them in their youth and, with more questionable motives, advertisers misled them in adult life." N W Pirie, *Food Resources Conventional and Novel* (Penguin 1969).
65. An *Observer* report (20 September 1992) presents research from eminent scientists who confirm that no infant feeding formula, and certainly not cow's milk, comes near to breast milk in its provision of fatty acids essential for the proper development of the brain.

SHORT BIBLIOGRAPHY

DIET AND LIFESTYLE

Geoffrey Cannon, *The Politics of Food*, Century 1988.
Peter Cox, *Why You Don't Need Meat*, Thorsons 1986.
Farhall, Lucas & Rofe, *Animal Free Shopper*, the Vegan Society.
Mark Gold, *Living Without Cruelty*, Green Print.
Michael Klaper, *Pregnancy, Children and the Vegan Diet*, available from The Vegan Society.
Gill Langley, *Vegan Nutrition*, The Vegan Society 1988.

ECOLOGY AND GENERAL

Jon Bennett and Susan George, *The Hunger Machine*, Polity Press 1987.
Kathleen Jannaway, *Abundant Living in the Coming Age of the Tree*, MCL.
Kenneth Melanby, *Can Britain Feed Itself?* Merlin 1975.
Ingrid Newkirk, *Save the Animals!* Angus & Robertson 1991.
Robert Sharpe, *The Cruel Deception*, Thorsons 1988 (on vivisection).
Jon Wynne-Tyson, *Food for a Future*, Thorsons 1988 (first published 1975).
Phil Wells & Mandy Jetter, *The Global Consumer*, Victor Gollancz 1991.

ANIMAL RIGHTS

Rebecca Hall, *Voiceless Victims,* Wildwood House 1984.

Tom Regan, *The Case for Animal Rights*, Routledge & Kegan Paul 1984.

Peter Singer, *Animal Liberation*, Thorsons 1985.

GARDENING

Kenneth Dalziel O'Brien, *Veganic Gardening,* Thorsons 1986.

Kathleen Jannaway, *Growing Our Own* — MCL booklet (see contacts).

RECOMMENDED COOKBOOKS

Eva Batt, *Vegan Cookery,* Thorsons reprint of an old classic.

Rose Elliot, *The Green Age Diet,* Fontana 1990.

Heather Lamont, *The Gourmet Vegan,* Gollancz 1988.

Leah Leneman, *The Single Vegan*, Thorsons 1989.

David Scott & Claire Golding, *The Vegan Diet,* Rider 1985.

David Scott, *Simply Vegan,* Thorsons 1992.

SOME USEFUL ADDRESSES

GENERAL ANIMAL RIGHTS

Animal Aid
The Old Chapel
Bradford Street
Tonbridge
Kent TN9 1AW

British Union for the Abolition of Vivisection
16a Crane Grove
Islington
London N7 8LB

National Anti-Vivisection Society
261 Goldhawk Road
London W12 9PE

Campaign for the Abolition of Angling
PO Box 130
Sevenoaks
Kent TN14 5NR

League Against Cruel Sports
83-87 Union Street
London SE1 1SG

Hunt Saboteurs Association
PO Box 1
Carlton
Nottingham NG4 2JY

DIET/LIFESTYLE

The Vegan Society
7 Battle Road
St Leonards on Sea
E Sussex TN37 7AA

Movement for Compassionate Living
47 Highlands Road
Leatherhead
Surrey KT22 8NQ

The Vegetarian Society
Parkdale
Dunham Road
Altrincham
Cheshire WA14 4QG

FACTORY FARMING

**Compassion in World
Farming**
20 Lavant Street
Petersfield
Hants GU32 3EW

GLOBAL CONCERN

Greenpeace
Greenpeace House
Canonbury Villas
London N1 2PN

Equal Exchange
29 Nicholson Street
Edinburgh EH8 9BX

Oxfam Trading
Murdoch Road
Bicester OX6 7RF

Traidcraft
Kingsway
Gateshead NE11 ONE

Baby Milk Action
23 St Andrew's Street
Cambridge CB2 3AX

NOTES

Also from Heretic Books

GREEN POLITICS

Sara Parkin
Green Parties: An International Guide   £7.95

Rudolf Bahro
Building the Green Movement   £6.95

Die Grünen
Programme of the German Green Party   £1.50

ANIMAL LIBERATION

William Johnson
The Rose-Tinted Menagerie   £8.95

William Johnson
The Monk Seal Conspiracy   £4.95

NORTH-SOUTH

Erik Dammann
Revolution in the Affluent Society   £5.95

Guy Brett
Through Our Own Eyes   £9.95

Please order where possible from your local bookshop or from:
Central Books, 99 Wallis Road, London E9 5LN.